# SOCIAL MEDIA

# SOCIAL MEDIA

# A Stage Play By
# Patrick M Benson

ISBN-13: 978-0692659922
ISBN-10: 0692659927

Library of Congress Control Number: 2016904288


BISAC: Performing Arts / Theater / General


Published by GO *-1, Flagstaff, Arizona, USA

For Paul Anthony Benson
3 Oct 1959 – 7 Apr 2016
with a brother's hope he has at last
found peace

# Cast of Characters

5 Male, 3 Female, 3 speaking Extras, 2-4 non-speaking Extras (see doubling notes)

**Joe**        Age 24, a soldier just returned home after serving two years in combat.

**Rita**        Age 24, Joe's girlfriend since high school, now his fiancé.

**George**        Age 24, a veteran who holds a grudge against Joe dating to their high school days.

**Roger**        Age 25, a fun-loving but dim-witted and malleable friend of George's. He has had an occasionally friendly relationship with Bill since their high school days.

**Bill**        Age 26, Rita's cousin, who has also had an on-and-off again relationship with Roger.

**<u>Chase</u>**     Age 25, Joe's best friend from high school who now holds a key Human Resources position at the local plant.

**<u>Emily</u>**     Age 24, Rita's co-worker, George's ex-lover, and long-term friend of both Joe and Rita.

**<u>Jessica</u>**     Age 22, former drug and alcohol abuser, she is George's current lover.

**<u>Bartender</u>**     Any age and either gender – may double as a non-speaking extra.

**<u>Officer</u>**     Any age and either gender – may double as a non-speaking extra.

**<u>Extras</u>**     Non-speaking actors appearing in bar and restaurant scenes but have no lines or significant action; may be doubled as noted above.

## **SETTING**

The play is contemporary, set in a small, Midwestern or Intermountain West, town.


## **TIME**

Most action occurs on a Tuesday morning through Friday evening. The final scene, a reconciliation, occurs about two weeks later.

## **STAGE**

The stage requires five areas.

1. An Apartment area with two rooms, a kitchen/living area and bedroom. The bedroom area must be large enough for a fight between husband and wife.
2. A Restaurant area that doubles as a diner and an American Legion Bar. It is suggested there should be three tables seating two, and a counter seating three.
3. An open area called the Street Scene where characters pass, meet and talk, and where significant physical action takes place. This can span a significant portion of the stage front.
4. An area between the Apartment and Restaurant that serves several uses.
   a. Coffee Shop that can be intimate. Must be visible to characters in the Street Scene.
   b. An HR Office and an adjoining hallway where characters wait and action occur. This has a typical office desk with chair, a visitor's chair and a door to the hallway.

# SCENES, CHANGES, INTERMISSION

## ACT I

Scene 1  Begins in the Apartment Set, transitions to the Street Scene, and ends in the Coffee Shop

## ACT II

Scene 1  Begins in the HR office, transitions to the American Legion Bar.

Scene 2  Begins in the American Legion Bar, transitions to the Street Scene, and ends in the Diner.

## ACT III

Scene 1  Begins in the Apartment Set, transitions to the Coffee Shop, and ends in the Street Scene

Scene 2  Begins in the HR Office, transitions to the American Legion Bar, and ends in the Street Scene.

Scene 3  Begins in the Diner and ends in the HR Office

Scene 4  Begins in the HR Office transitions in order to the American Legion Bar, the Street Scene, Diner, the Apartment Set, back to the Street Scene, and finally ends in the Apartment Set

Scene 5  The Diner (two weeks later)

## Scene Changes

Scene changes within Acts are as
flowing as practical, rather than a
stop … stage reset … restart action.
Naturally this is given limitations
of the stage and company.

## Intermission

A single intermission would be
logical between Act 2 and Act 3.

**ACT I**
**Scene 1**

Setting:   JOE and RITA are in bed in
           the Apartment Set. It is
           morning just before their
           alarm would ring.

           In the Coffee Shop, GEORGE
           and BILL sit at a table.
           The lights are half-up
           there, dim but not dark.
           Initially the actors move
           slowly, apparently
           drinking coffee and
           talking. There is no
           speaking and nothing
           should be done overtly to
           attract attention to this
           area of the stage.

At Rise:   Lights come up in the
           Apartment Set where JOE
           and RITA are in bed. JOE
           is waking from a
           nightmare.


                    JOE
           (Yelling and trashing in
           bed)
Smitty! There! At your 2! At your 2!
Six of them at your 2! Moving right!
No! … No! … There! Damn it! Pauly!
Pauly, at your 10! Get 'em! Hit 'em!
Hit them there! There! Get them!
Christ! Get them!

                    RITA
Joe … Joe … honey … Joe … baby …
it's all right now. You're OK.
You're safe now.

                    JOE
          (Swings elbow towards Rita,
          hitting her in the face.)
No! No! No!

                    RITA
          (Grabs nose.)
Oh! Ouch!
          (Rolls away. Nose is
          bleeding. Gets out of bed.
          Puts tissue or cloth to her
          nose to stop the bleeding.)

                    JOE
          (Bolts out of bed)
Shit! Rita, did I get you again? Is
it bad? Are you bleeding? Here …
here's a tissue.

                    RITA
You were having a nightmare. Yelling
at Smitty and Pauly.

                    JOE
Yeah. It was one about the night the
Haj came through the wire. Sorry. I
don't know what triggers it. I …

                    RITA
Don't worry, honey. The folks at the
Army spouse's briefing said you'd

(RITA Continued)
probably have those for a while.
Dreams, I mean.

                    JOE
I'm so sorry. Let me look at your
nose. Looks like you've bled through
that one. Let me get you a new one.
          (Gets RITA another
          tissue)
That's what they told us, too. Wish
they'd told me how long they'd last.
It's been two months since I rotated
stateside; and I've been home a week
already.
          (Gently, lovingly, daubs
          blood from RITA'S nose.)
For what it's worth it's only a
flesh wound that probably won't kill
you. I've seen worse. Let me kiss it
and make it better.
          (Kisses RITA's nose)

                    RITA
That's good medicine.
          (Daubs nose.)
Look, it's stopped already.
          (Beat)
Cut yourself some slack, Joe. You've
only been home a few days. Go back
to bed. You don't need to get up
yet.

                    JOE
Sure. Sorry again. Maybe the VA
folks will be able to help. They
have a walk-in sick call clinic

                    (JOE Continued)
every day at 1100. I'll go there
today.

                    RITA
That's a good idea. I mean … if you
want to, that is. They said we
shouldn't push you guys too much.
I'm not pushing too much … am I?

                    JOE
Too much?

                    RITA
Yes, silly. The Chaplin said we
should encourage and engage but do
not force or threaten. Those were
his exact words.
          (Looks at clock)
Joe, honey, its time I was up! Be my
hero and make me a piece of toast
while I clean up and get dressed.

                    JOE
Sure thing, babe.

          (Exit RITA - costume change)

                    JOE
          (Takes a small package from
          a bedside drawer)
It's probably is time to give her
this.
          (JOE Moves to kitchen area,
          pours juice and starts
          toast)

(Enter RITA into kitchen, dressed for school, carrying a backpack and a garment bag.)

(Once in the kitchen, RITA puts down the bags and stands close to JOE.)

JOE
Bleeding still stopped?

RITA
Pretty much. You caught me pretty good this time.

JOE
Kiss and make up?

RITA
What do you think?

(RITA and JOE kiss passionately)

RITA
Hold it big guy. I need to stay focused today. I've got my very last final exam this morning and corporate recruiters are on campus today. The last thing I need on my mind is you and me horizontal!

JOE
Rats! At least I know I still can get you hot and bothered!

                              RITA
                    (Takes JOE'S hands and
                    places them on her breasts)
          These girls have been all yours and
          yours alone, babe. They've been
          under wraps for two years, just
          waiting for you to come home.


                              JOE
          You have no idea how glad I am to
          hear that some things haven't
          changed. Lots of guys get bad
          surprises when they get home. When
          they warned you about nightmares
          they were warning us about different
          kinds of nightmares.
                    (Hands RITA breakfast)
          Here's your breakfast.
                    (RITA and JOE eat while they
                    speak)
          Ready for those exams?


                              RITA
                    (Eating and talking)
          Yes, I've got most of it down cold.
          This last exam is a comprehensive
          one. More to be sure you did your
          own work over the last couple of
          years.


                              JOE
          Some folks cheat?


                              RITA
          You bet! Some folks will do anything
          to get an advantage.

                    JOE
Huh, why would someone do that? It's
not like you can fake the work even
if cheating gets you in the door.
Here.
          (JOE hands RITA the package)
I brought this back for you. I've
been waiting for a good time to give
it to you.

                    RITA
          (Opens package, finding an
          ornate cuff-type bracelet)
Oh, Joe, it's beautiful! You didn't
have to bring me anything.
          (Puts on the bracelet)
Where did you get it?


                    JOE
They sell this type of thing at the
markets over there. The men value
themselves by how much jewelry they
can wrap around their women.

                    RITA
And girlfriends, too, I bet.

                    JOE
No! Never. That would be too
forward. Any woman who would accept
jewelry from a man outside her
immediate family would be seen as a
whore!

                    RITA
          (Moves close to JOE)
What does all this mean?

                    JOE
            (Lovingly holds RITA'S
            wrist)
See this? It represents the return
of the warrior. This script here
talks about Suleiman's victories and
his righteousness. He was a biggie
in their history.

                    RITA
Well, whatever it is, I love it.
Thank you, babe. I know it will give
me good luck today.
            (RITA plays with bracelet,
            then passionately kisses
            JOE)
Now … I've got to get going. I want
to have time to meet with as many of
those recruiters as possible.

I just wish there were more decent
job openings here in town. Are you
going to see Chase today?

                    JOE
Yeah. I need to start looking for a
job. I've been home a week already
and I'm going stir crazy just
sitting around this apartment.

When I'm here alone the walls start
talking to me. They rise up and
accuse me of malingering and living
off your waitressing tips.

                    RITA
Babe! You're not living off me. You
needed to take a few days to get
used to how things are back here.
The folks at that briefing said
that, too.


                    JOE
Yeah, I know that. It's just that
you're finishing college and
interviewing for these high-powered
jobs. All I get to do is talk to
Chase about a first-level supervisor
jobs.


                    RITA
Don't put yourself down. You did a
damn good job in the Army. Look at
those medals. Even Daddy was
impressed! Purple Hearts and a
Bronze Star! He said they don't just
issue those with the combat boots.
He's been telling everyone he knows
that you're a real hero. Chase said
the same thing, too.


                    JOE
Glad he thinks so.


                    RITA
Joseph Andrew Williams I won't hear
you put yourself down! Only you and
George Weber had the balls to join
the Army, and he was a clerk at Fort
Campbell his whole time. You were in
combat for two years.

(RITA Continued)
Joe … babe … you did a hell of a
lot. Chase told me the new
management really wants you to work
with them.

                    JOE
But you're interviewing for a job
that might make use move? Even if I
get a job here? Don't you think
that's a cheap-ass thing to do to
Chase?

                    RITA
When … and if … I get some great job
offer in Omaha or Minneapolis … or
Timbuktu for that matter … we can
talk about it then.

No. You … we … need to do what's
best for us. When we get settled …
whether it is here or some big city
… then we can get married and start
a family.

                    JOE
But I'd feel like I owed Chase if he
offered me a job or something.

                    RITA
You've got it backwards, babe. You
don't owe this town anything. It's
the other way around. You've just
come back from war. Things changed
while you were gone.

(RITA Continued)
In my business classes I've learned
it's that corporate commitment to
the community or workers disappeared
when the economy tanked in '07.

                    JOE
Yeah! It looks like most of the mom-
and-pop stores in town are boarded
up now.

                    RITA
A lot of folks here have been hurt.
No doubt about that. But the plant
was bought out and automated instead
of being closed up. Most folks got
to keep their jobs.

As bad as it's been … my Dad, your
Uncle, Chase, Roger and Bill … all
the people we knew back in high
school … even that marginal
performer Jessica … all of them at
the plant … got to keep their jobs.

                    JOE
I understand all that Rita. You've
got to see it from my perspective.
How will these people really feel
when they see a vet like me come
waltzing back into town and taking
job from someone who has been
working hard towards it for years?

Do you really think their patriotic
spirit will go that far?

(JOE Continued)
And … as far as a new management
team at the plant goes … I hear
George hasn't found a job yet.

RITA
A couple weeks ago Chase told me
George interviewed a couple of times
and nobody was impressed enough to
hire him. All of them thought
something just wasn't quite right.
Apparently George hasn't changed at
all.

JOE
You're talking a lot about Chase
now. Should I be worried?

RITA
No! Babe, we all grew up together!
You and me … Chase and Roger and my
cousin Bill, and even George … we've
known each other since grade school!
I see Chase and Joanne at the
restaurant every Monday night when
they bring their girls in for
burgers and lemon pie. ... And Bill
and Roger are there most Thursdays.

I really can't stay and talk about
this now. I've got to get going.

JOE
Yeah, I guess so.

                    RITA
Joe … I know you're having a tough
time. Don't be depressed. Remember,
most of the folks from around here
like you, still believe in you, know
you've done good things for your
country and feel you should be
rewarded for it. Trust them and not
those demons you're carrying in your
head. And remember that I love you
more than anything. Ok?


                    JOE
Ok. Can we take it up again tonight?

                    RITA
             (Picking up the school
             and clothes bags.)
Yes! I'll call after my exam and
tell you how it went. Now, big guy,
give me a kiss and go get dressed. I
bought you a blue striped shirt to
wear to the interviews today. It
looks professional and the color
brings out the blue in your eyes.


             (RITA sets down both her
             school and clothes bags,
             goes to JOE and they kiss,
             not as passionately as
             earlier.)

             (Exit RITA - Carrying
             school bag but leaving her
             clothes bag.)

                    JOE
          (Walks to the bedroom,
          picks up the new shirt
          and, while putting it on,
          miss-buttons it and
          becomes frustrated.)
Combat hero … shit … wish I'd been a
damn clerk like George. Bet he
doesn't have nightmares. Tired of …
          (Realizes he's miss-
          buttoned the shirt.
          Explodes in anger. Rips
          shirt off, scattering the
          buttons. Sits down on
          bed.)
… <u>this fucking shirt!</u>

          (Enter RITA - Comes into
          the bedroom talking.

                    RITA
Joe … can you believe I forgot my
interview and work clothes. What was
I thinking?
          (Sees JOE with the damaged
          shirt. Is startled.)
Oh, Joe … babe. What happened?

                    JOE
Oh, fuck, Rita. I'm sorry.
          (Angry at himself)
I fucked up putting on the fucking
shirt. Then I just blew up. Looks
like I ruined it. Let me pick up
these buttons.

                    RITA
            (Gently touching Joe's
            shoulder and back)
Babe, don't worry about it. Calm
down, babe. They're just a bunch of
buttons.

                    JOE
Simple fucking shirt and I couldn't
even do that right! How the hell am
I going to get a job let alone keep
one? I can't even fucking button a
shirt … can't even dress myself.

And you and your good buddy Chase
expect me to tell people how to do
things! Are the two of you going to
fix my nightmares? Fix these shakes
I get? Fix the damn shirt. Maybe you
two can fix the rest of me while
you're at it?

                    RITA
Joe! Damn it! You're yelling about
something other than a shirt. Aren't
you? I can see that. Babe! Come on!
I can see you're upset.

Is it a my-job versus your-job
thing? Because if it is we need to
talk about it; and there's no time
right now. I've got to get to
school, take my exam, and maybe,
just maybe, score an interview so I
can get a better job away from this
small town!

                    JOE
What you have isn't a good enough
job? From the way you were talking
about folks in town I thought many
of them would jump at a job like
yours!

                    RITA
Quit playing word games, Joe! You
know what I mean. I've busted my ass
over the last four years … lived
with my folks … gone to college …
got good grades … worked six days a
week … waited for you to come home …
and done a damn good job of it all.
What gives you the right to come
back now and treat me this way!

                    JOE
I don't know. I can see you've done
it all and I've just come back. And
now I'm sticking my nose in
everything. Sorry.

                    RITA
We don't have time for this. Lets
get you another shirt so you can get
to your meeting with Chase and I can
get to school.
                    (RITA passes a less
                    fashionable, even gaudy,
                    shirt to JOE)
Here, try this one on.

                    JOE
Christ, Rita, I'm sorry I screwed
up. It was just …

(JOE buttons the second
shirt as RITA watches)

RITA

Don't worry about it now. We can fix
it later.

JOE
(Quickly finishes
putting on the shirt
and getting ready.)
How's this look?

RITA

It's OK. Now, I'm late. I've got to
go or I'll miss my bus.

JOE

Let me walk with you there. I made
you late and the least I can do now
is carry your gear. I'll go to the
VA later today and see if they can
help me.

RITA   (Cheerfully)
That's a good idea. They're set up
for that. … Kiss me before we go.
For love and luck!

(RITA and JOE kiss)

(RITA and JOE moved from
the Apartment Set to the
Street Scene.)

(Apartment Lights Dim)

(Street Scene Lights Up)

(Coffee Shop Lights
Up)

            RITA
Don't be obvious, but look over
there … in the coffee shop … George
and Bill. Wonder what they're up to
now?

            JOE
If memory serves me, George <u>was</u>
quite a crap-head in school.

            RITA
That is true. I hear his parents
have pretty much disowned him.
Nobody but him knows why.
          (Looks across the stage.)
Here comes my bus.

            JOE
          (Hands RITA the gear he is
          carrying for her.)
And I'll bet he isn't telling
anyone.

            GEORGE
Bill, look over there. Good old Joe
and Rita.
          (Ridiculing)
Don't they make just the prettiest
couple?

(GEORGE Continued)
The war hero with his cheerleader.
The walking cliché.

> (JOE and RITA kiss - as
> much for passion as to
> make a point to BILL and
> GEORGE in the coffee shop)

> (Exit RITA, carrying her
> schoolbooks and work
> clothes)

> (Exit JOE, in a different
> direction than RITA but
> should pass within sight
> of the Coffee Shop)

> (BILL looks at the couple
> walking. Nods with a
> considered pause.)

                    BILL
Yeah. Get a look at that shirt.
Wonder who picked it out … Rita or
him? Word at the plant is that he's
a shoe-in for a supervisor position
that opened up last week. A bunch of
us who've been there years got
pushed out in the cold.

                  GEORGE
Really? A supervisory position? Last
week Chase told me there weren't
even any production-line positions
open. I wonder what's happened since
then?

                    BILL
The new management team announced
they want to offer any open
positions to returning combat vets
first. Hell, George, you meet that
criteria, too? Don't you? You did
your time in combat, too. Didn't
you?

                  GEORGE
Yeah. Guess so. Except that those
two, Joe and his best buddy Chase,
have had it in for me since high
school.
              (Beat)
Remember how those two went to the
coach and had me benched for most of
our senior year? I called Joe out on
it in front of the whole damn
coaching staff. Remember how they
all blew me off?

                    BILL
              (Avoids eye contact with
              GEORGE)
Yeah. I remember.

                  GEORGE
Wish I knew what I did back then to
piss them off. That jerk Joe and his
sidekick Chase have kept me under
their thumbs ever since. And don't
you remember - the word at school
was they were gay.

                    BILL
I don't know if he's gay or not.
Rita seems happy enough with him.
She's always going on about how good
a guy he is. And he did win a Bronze
Star for valor.

                  GEORGE
Maybe, maybe … but I still think
those must have something going on.
Like I said, just last week Chase
told me there weren't any job
openings anywhere at the plant and
you know as well as me that I meet
their new criteria. He said there
weren't any openings on the horizon
even. Now we hear Joe's in line for
one. And, not just a line job, but
one as a supervisor! How's that
happen if there's not something
going on? … You answer me that.

                    BILL
Who knows about Chase, man? Not me.
Like I said, word is out that the
new owners want to hire returning
combat vets. I had a formal
interview with Chase last week. He
told me then that there were a
couple of openings and that likely I
had one of them in the bag. Then,
yesterday, he comes up all
apologetic-like and says they're off
the table. And now this comes along
just for Joe. Maybe you should talk
with Chase again. Maybe things
changed last week.

GEORGE
Maybe … Maybe I will. But if I find
Chase or Joe cut me out again I'll
be hard pressed not to do something
about it. Sometimes you have to even
the playing field with assholes.


BILL
Yeah, I know what you mean. Word is
that some of Rita's family has never
really liked the idea of her and Joe
together. And, I've been working my
ass off at the plant for five years.
Now that a management slot opens up
I'm being held down because I wasn't
in the Army.
          (Beat)
What do you have in mind by even the
playing field?


GEORGE
How do you feel about pretending to
be Joe and posting messages as him
on-line? You can post things that
make it appear he's looking for
someone new to do the nasty with.
When we have a good thread going we
can share it with Rita. She'll dump
Joe faster than yesterday's tacos.


BILL
That might work.
          (Pause)
Yeah. Hell, yes. Count me in.

                        GEORGE
Good! I'll set up a bogus profile
for Joe and send the link and
password to you. I'll build one for
Rita and pretend to be her.
                (Beat)
And I'll take your advice and talk
to Chase again, too.

                        BILL
Speaking of Chase, I've got to get
to work. When I get the link I'll
get started on it. I'll have some
time during my shift today. Thanks
for the coffee.


                        (Enter ROGER - As he
                        enters, ROGER bumps into
                        BILL. They exchange an old
                        lover's glance. GEORGE
                        notices the glance.)

                        ROGER
Hey, Bill. Sorry about that. Get any
on you?

                        BILL
No, but it was close. Catch you
later?

                        ROGER
Sure.

                        (Exit BILL)

                    GEORGE
Hey, Roger, grab a seat! Let me buy
you a cup.

                    ROGER
OK, only if you make it one to go.
I'm running late for work.

                    GEORGE
          (Motions and calls to some
          unseen barista)
Can we get another one here. And,
make it to go. Thanks!
          (Beat)
Speaking of work … I just heard
there's a supervisory position open.
You hear anything about it?

                    ROGER
Hell, yes, I heard about it! Got
fucked over about it, too. I went to
HR and interviewed with Chase last
week. He said there were two
positions and that I had a good
chance of landing one of them.

Then he calls me yesterday and says
the positions have been closed. Says
the new management team has their
eye on outside candidates. On top of
that … I hear they want the new guys
on board by Friday. Friday! For
God's sake, where are they going to
get someone by Friday?

                    GEORGE
I'll tell you how.

(GEORGE Continued)
They can get them here if that
outside candidate is our old friend
Joe ... fresh back in town and
already throwing his weight around.
Just like back in high school.

ROGER
What! Why? Shit! That asshole Joe
doesn't know squat about plant
business. What a smart ass! Makes me
want to smack him one in the face.
See what he could do … just me and
him … one-on-one, without Chase or
military backup.

GEORGE
That's sort of what Bill said, too.
          (Plotting and smiling.)
Roger, here's a thought. I'm not
sure what you'll think. This is a
stream of consciousness thing. How
would you feel about pretending to
be Rita on a social media site? I
could play Joe looking for love in
all the wrong places, while you
pretend to be Rita all heart-broken,
claiming to be waiting at home for
him, but missing all her old lovers.
          (Beat)
We can make it look like she's
figured Joe is a player planning to
dump her and she's decided to dump
his sorry ass first. Then we can
share the whole thing with everyone
… or just laugh our asses off at
them both.

                    BILL
Good idea, George. Good idea. Count
me in. It'll serve that son-of-a-
bitch and his fuck-buddy gal-pal
right.

                    GEORGE
I'll set up a profile and send you
the link and password.

                    BILL
Here's my card. My email address is
on it.
          (Stands at table)
Now, I gotta' get to work. Don't
want to be late. Don't want to give
anyone a reason to chew me out,
again.

          (Exit BILL)

                    GEORGE
          (Laughs while speaking as
          he types on a laptop)
This will take good old trusting Joe
down a bit.

He's always trusted people who seem
honest … whether they deserve it or
not …

Rita and Chase and Roger and Bill …
and me, too, for all that matters.
Joe trusts Rita more than he trusts
himself. This will cut him deep and
wide on that trust.

(GEORGE Continued)
Making her seem like she's cheated
will confuse him at the very least.
But, I bet he's carrying some combat
stress, and that will compound the
confusion and make him act a bit …
rashly.

Maybe I can help him focus that
rashness so maybe … just maybe … he
works himself out of a job. And,
maybe out of Rita, too. That would
be so choice … helping him out of
that relationship. That would get
him to leave town forever.

Roger and Bill, my gay old friends.
You don't need to know you're
playing opposite sides of the same
coin. I'll let you think the other
side is me. When all this is done
everyone will have a good hard laugh
and realize that good old trusting
Joe is nothing more than a blind and
dumb idiot. Nobody will care, in the
end anyway, who played which role.
        (Typing with gusto)

There. Done. A profile of Joe for
Roger and a profile of Rita for
Bill. This will be fun. Bill as Joe
looking for a booty call, and Roger
as Rita cheating on Joe. And no one
but me knowing I'm playing them
against each. Playing them like
fish.
        (Mocking laugh)

(GEORGE Continued)

Now, George, let's us set up some
plausible deniability with a quick
text message to that good old
trusting idiot.

(Types)

Hey, Joe. Saw you with Rita this
morning. From one vet to another,
welcome home. Word on the street is
you're meeting with Chase about jobs
at the plant. Before you jump into
the wide-world-o-work how about we
meet for lunch and a beer or two at
the Legion Hall? My treat. We can
swap war stories and I can bring you
up to speed on VA benefits and
opportunities to be paid a lot for
doing a little or nothing at all. No
reason for you to start a new grind
so quick! 1300 today work for you?

(Mocking laugh)


CURTAIN

-- END OF ACT I --

## **ACT II**
## **Scene 1**

Setting:   JOE stands in the hallway
          outside the door to
          CHASE's office in the HR
          Office Set.

          In the American Legion
          Bar, the actors, including
          GEORGE and EXTRAS move
          slowly, as if orders are
          being placed and drinks
          served, but there is no
          talking and nothing should
          be done to attract
          attention to this area of
          the stage.

At Rise:   Lights are fully up in the
          HR Office. JOE is nervous,
          pacing the hallway,
          preparing to meet and
          review job opportunities
          at the plant.

                    JOE
          (Removes phone from pocket
          and speaks to himself.)
First rule of the successful
interview … take no texts or calls.
          (Looks at phone.)
Oh, a message from George.
          (Reading aloud the message
          that George was typing at
          the end of Act 1)

                    (JOE Continued)
How about we meet for lunch and a
beer or two at the Legion Hall? My
treat.
                    (Beat)
Yada … Yada … Yada
                    (Beat)
No reason for you to start a new
grind so quick! 1300 today work for
you?
                    (Beat)
Huh? A welcome home from George.
                    (Beat)
Guess that works for me.
                    (Quickly answers message.
                    Pockets phone. Knocks on
                    door.)

                    CHASE
                    (Opens door. Sincerely
                    shakes Joe's hand.)
Joe! Glad you could make it. It's
good to see you home and in one
piece! Have a chair and let's chat
for a bit.
                    (CHASE moves behind the
                    desk, JOE in front of it.)
Let me cut right to it. I'm sure
you've heard about the new
management team here at the plant. A
new management team means a new set
of staffing rules for the HR team.

They've tasked me to seek out
returning combat vets for open
positions. That's why I reached out
to you.

(CHASE Continued)
There are two opportunities here
that have your name written all over
them. Here, look these over and tell
me what you think.

(CHASE passes folders with
job descriptions to JOE)

JOE
Thanks! The economy being what it is
I appreciate even being considered.
How'd you know I was available?

CHASE
Rita told me. Me and Joanne and the
girls run into her at the restaurant
when we eat out. And we bump into
each other at the supermarket every
couple of weeks or so. She's been
keeping us up to date on what you've
been doing.
(Smiles, laughs)
Got to tell you, Joe. She's your
biggest fan.

JOE
Glad to hear that!

CHASE
You should be. Now, let's get to it.
I've been authorized to offer you
either of two positions we have open
right now. The first one is a Shop
Floor Entry-Level Supervisor; a good
fit today but one without a lot of
upward potential.

                    (CHASE Continued)
The second is an Assistant Office
Manager. Both start immediately, as
in today, if you want.

                    JOE
Wow, that's quick!
                    (Looks over the papers.)
Jeeze, Chase, I don't know which I'd
be best qualified for. The Shop
Floor job is interesting, but it
looks like the Assistant Office
Manager one has more potential.
Which would you advise me to take?

                    CHASE
Pick the one that lights your fire?
Business works different than
government, Joe. Here, you can try
one and if it doesn't fit well you
can change. Management has tasked me
to on-board vets ASAP. That
recommendation will be you and only
you. But, we need to move
immediately … this week if possible.

                    JOE
                    (Looking at and shuffling
                    the papers)
I'd like to go over these
possibilities with my biggest fan.
If you know what I mean.

                    CHASE
That's probably a good idea. You and
Rita are a strong team.
                    (Beat)

(CHASE Continued)
And, you don't want to screw with a good deal! Like I said, one way or the other, you need to let me know ASAP which job you'd like. Today is Tuesday and I need to forward a name by Friday at the latest. That gives you a couple days to decide.

                    JOE
Rita is taking her final exams today. And after that she has a shift at the diner.
                    (Beat)
In all honesty, Chase, I've got to tell you something. There are recruiters on campus that Rita wants to talk with. They might offer her something out of town.

                    CHASE
Rita told me that, too.
                    (Beat)
Everyone would understand if she gets an out-of-town offer and you both hit the road.

                    JOE
So the best I can promise you is tomorrow. OK?

                    CHASE
One-Way or the other that should work. Thanks for coming in so soon after your return stateside. Me and Joanne would like to have the two of you over, just to talk.

(CHASE Continued)
No big rush, but we'd like you to
meet the girls and they'd like to
meet you.
                (Pensively)
I know a lot of guys want to take a
vacation. Those who take a long one
do run the risk of losing career
momentum. For Rita's and your future
sakes don't do that.


                    JOE
I'll get back with you.
                (JOE and CHASE shake
                hands.)
Thanks again, Chase. We worked well
back in school and I think we'll
work well now.


            (Exit JOE)

            (HR Office Lights Dim)

            (Exit CHASE - slowly)

            (American Legion Bar
            Lights Up)


                    GEORGE
Bartender! Give me two tall cold
ones. I'm expecting a friend.
                (Looks towards American
                Legion door)
Ah! Here he is now.

                    (Enter JOE - Waves at
                    GEORGE and takes seat next
                    to him.)

                         JOE
Hey. How's it going?

                      GEORGE
Not bad, Joe, not bad at all.
                    (Beers arrive)
I bought you a cold one. Welcome
home, soldier. Cheers!

                    (GEORGE and JOE tip
                    glasses)

                      GEORGE
I heard you were interviewing at the
plant. How'd that go?

                         JOE
                    (Sips beer and considers
                    answer)
I don't know. I'm not convinced that
the plant's the best place for me.
Maybe I'm not in as big a hurry as
Chase wants me to be.

                      GEORGE
I know what you mean. I talked with
him a while ago … back when I
separated from the Army. He pushed
back when I said I needed some time
to get my head back around living in
town again.

                    JOE
I'd heard you'd joined up. What was
your M.O.S.?

                    GEORGE
11B. You?

                    JOE
Same. Made E-6 over in the sandpit.
How'd you do?

                    GEORGE
E-5. Redlined from E-6 when I
wouldn't re-up.

                    JOE
Know how that goes. Did you see much
action?

                    GEORGE
                (Evasively)
Nothing to jump up and down about. I
hear you saw some shit.

                    JOE
Yeah. Did back-to-backs in Iraq and
the 'Stan. Lots of fun. You?

                    GEORGE
                (Dodging admitting he
                stayed stateside during
                his four-year term of
                service.)
Hmmm.
                (Waves to bartender.)
Let me buy your lunch.

                    JOE
          (Looks at George as if
          something is not quite
          right.)
Sure.

          (American Legion Bar
          Lights Dim.)

## ACT II
## Scene 2

Setting:    GEORGE and JOE are finishing lunch in the American Legion Bar,.

At Rise:    GEORGE picks up the conversation in mid sentence.


GEORGE
(Picks up conversation)
… So, like I was saying, Joe, there's no reason to be in big a hurry. You don't have to take the first job that comes along. There are federal and state programs for returning vets, and a cushy VA Disability program that will pay about the same as you were making over in the sandpit; well, 80% of it at least.

What you need to do is take some time, get your feet under you before moving forward. Register and visit with the VA. Get reacquainted with Rita. Visit your families. Look up your buddies. Borrow a boat and go fishing. You've been gone from here six years and I can guarantee you that things have changed in ways you don't know and can't imagine.

                    JOE
I know what you mean. One thing is
different … before I went into the
Army the plant HR folks wouldn't
give me the time of day. This
morning I met with Chase and he
offered me a couple positions.

                  GEORGE
Yeah, and I bet he said you had to
take one right quick. Didn't he? He
wants to get corporate hooks into
your tender young ass before you
figure out there's more out there
than working in the plant.

                    JOE
Well, yes. He did do that. But …

                  GEORGE
But … what? They're manipulating
you, Joe. Can't you see? Don't do
it. Not yet, anyway. They want to
trap you because you're worth more
as their worker-bee than working for
a competitor. Be your own man, Joe.
They're afraid if you take time and
look around you'll see that what
they want is in their bets interest.
It's damn sure not in yours or
Rita's.

                    JOE
That may be.
          (Beat - thinking)

                    (JOE Continued)
What happened to you in the Army?
When did you turn into this, "Don't
tread on me" type of guy? Back in
the day you were a go-along-to-get-
along person.


                    GEORGE
I guess the Army helped me figure
out that nobody is ever going to
look out for me and better than me.


                    JOE
Since when have I been in your
family? The last time we did
anything together was back in high
school. And then, you spent half our
senior year blaming me and Chase for
getting cut from the football team.


                    GEORGE
I don't blame you … not now anyway.
          (Beat)
I figured it was when I called out a
couple of fags I caught doing the
nasty in the locker room. Told the
Coach it was them or me. Ended up
being me.
          (Beat)
And, anyway, that was a long time
ago. Another life. We've both been
in the Army and that changed us.
Both of us.
          (Beat)
I just want you to think about the
plant and Chase and how these two
opportunities just happened to

(GEORGE Continued)
magically drop in your lap. Why do
you think that happened? Why just
for you? Maybe they have something
else up their corporate sleeve?
          (Beat)
Did you really expect this?
          (Beat)
I got out and came back here almost
a year ago. I interviewed at the
plant, too … with Chase, too … got
called in five or six times. And,
buddy, let me tell you, nothing came
of all my efforts … not a goddamn
thing.
          (Beat)
What has changed? Chase is telling
you the same things he told me back
then. You and I have similar
experiences and qualifications. Why
is he laying these positions at your
feet? Could it be you're facing a
world of other opportunities and he
doesn't want you to look at them?


                    JOE
I don't know, George. Chase says
that there's a new management team
and they...


                  GEORGE
New Management, my ass! Hell, man.
My resume is still on file and they
haven't been calling me about them.
And what about Bill and Roger?
They've been working at the plant
since we graduated from high school.

                    (GEORGE Continued)
You know that Chase told them about
these positions, and got them stoked
up about them. Then he pulled the
rug out from beneath them. Suddenly
his story changes from promoting
long-term employees to bringing in
vets. But he doesn't call me. He
knows I'm a vet, too. And now he's
pushing talk about some new
management team. What's that?

                    JOE
I don't know. Seriously. This is the
first I've heard about Bill and
Roger losing out.

                    GEORGE
I'd have bet you a beer, maybe two,
that Chase wouldn't have mentioned
it. He never does.

     (GEORGE and JOE finish eating.)

                    JOE
I've got to get going. The beer and
lunch were a good idea. What's my
share?

                    GEORGE
I paid the bill earlier. I'll walk
with you.

                    (GEORGE and JOE walk away
                    from the American Legion
                    Bar onto the Street Scene)

(American Legion Bar
Lights Dim)

(Street Scene Lights Up)

                    GEORGE
Do you two have any plans now that
Rita is graduating?

                    JOE
She's hoping one of her professors
to grease the skids so she gets an
interview. Not sure what will come
of it. She's staying working at the
restaurant until something firms up.

                    GEORGE
I know. My ex works there, too. You
remember Emily, don't you?

                    JOE
Yes, I'd heard you two weren't a
couple any more. Sorry to hear you
broke up. What happened?

                    GEORGE
She wants to get her sweet ass out
of this town and I don't know that I
share that opinion.

                    JOE
                 (Looks at GEORGE as if to
                 ask a question but is
                 interrupted by BILL and
                 ROGER Entry.)

                    (Enter ROGER and BILL -
                    the four meet at mid
                    stage)

                        GEORGE
                    (Is not happy to see Roger
                    and Bill together)

                        ROGER
Hey, there are two of our favorite
combat vets.
                    (Genuinely interested)
Joe, when you get settled I'd like
to buy you a beer and hear some of
your stories. George says the two of
you had similar experiences. My
grandfather was in the Army back in
the day. He used to spin stories
like George does. I'd like to hear
some of yours.

                        JOE
                    (Looks at GEORGE, knowing
                    he was never in combat.)
Yeah, maybe someday we'll do that.
Not sure if our experiences are …

                        GEORGE
Our experiences won't be the same,
Roger. Joe's experiences are higher
on the "seen-some-shit" scale.
                    (Beat)
Isn't that right, Joe? Even GI's who
serve in the same unit … even guys
fighting side-by-side … experience
things differently. Don't we, Joe?

                    JOE
          (Reluctant to call out a
          fellow vet for lying.)
Yeah. I guess so.
          (Beat)
Hey guys, George tells me Chase
talked to both of you about those
open jobs. I hope you don't hold it
against me if I follow up on one of
them. Those are about the only work
I've seen here in town. I can't see
myself sitting around drawing
disability and unemployment waiting
for shit to happen. Rita wants to
start a family and I don't think she
wants to wait much longer.


                  ROGER
          (Dejected)
This town hasn't changed much. And
you can always go to school like
George and Rita.


                  JOE
School would be better than nothing.
Maybe you're right about this being
the same small town. Maybe it's me
that's changed. Maybe it's that all
of us have changed.
          (Looks at his phone.)
Sorry, guys, I've got to get going.
Just got a text from Rita saying
she's finished her exams and I want
to surprise her.

(Exit JOE - giving GEORGE
"the look" that veterans
with combat experience
give vets who stayed
stateside)

GEORGE
Well … that was a quick exit? I'm
not sure if he's in a bigger hurry
to screw Rita or screw you guys out
of a job.

ROGER
Yeah, rubbing our noses in his good
fortune. Right now what I'd like to
do is adjust his nose, that's what
I'd like to do.

BILL
Roger, let it go. It wasn't his
fault.

ROGER
And what was with that look he shot
you?

GEORGE
What look? I didn't see any look.
Anyway, I don't know what's going on
with him. He can be a fucking
asshole from time to time.
(Beat)
Well guys, I've got to get going.
Catch you later.

(Exit BILL and ROGER in
one direction, GEORGE in
another)

(Street Scene Lights Dim)

(Diner Lights Up)

(ENTER RITA and EMILY
enter, carrying supplies
for setting the counter
for a dinner crowd. They
enter continuing a
conversation.

                RITA
… And the starting salaries are in
the low 60's with raises based on
semi-annual reviews.

                EMILY
They can actually promise all that?
What could be better? A private
office … lots of money … health care
paid for … and a real retirement?
Oh, Rita, right now I'm not sure if
I'm more happy for you or envious of
you.

            RITA (Laughing)
Don't be either, not yet anyway.
I've just had the first interview.
If they're really interested in me
they'll call later today and set up
a second meeting. That's the money
meeting.

                    (Pause as RITA and EMILY
                    work)

                         EMILY
                    (Serious)
How's our boy today?


                         RITA
Joe is pretty screwed up right now.
I'm not sure if he's up for the
insecurity of moving again. You
know, so soon after coming back from
the war and getting out of the Army.


                         EMILY
Girlfriend, don't underestimate that
man. If anyone can do it, Joe can.


                         RITA
I appreciate your confidence. Chase
interviewed him this morning.
There're a couple of positions at
the plant, and Chase told me the new
management team wants to fill them
with returning vets. He says they're
positioning the plant to transition
when the war ends.


                         EMILY
George interviewed with Chase
earlier this year. I'm not sure if
it was Chase, but someone on the
interview team saw George for the
self-serving, lying, SOB he is.

                    RITA
How'd that work out for him? He
doesn't seem to be working.

                    EMILY
They turned him down. George sure
was pissed about it.
          (Beat)
About then we split up. Now, his
thing is to spend his mornings at
school and afternoons at the Legion
Hall bar. He's milking the system
for all he can get and whining about
those who are getting ahead.

                    RITA
George spoke with Joe about meeting
for lunch there today.

                    EMILY
I'd nip that one in the bud if I
were you. George is a taker not a
giver; and, I remember Joe as a
trusting guy.

                    RITA
He still is … sometimes too much so.
I'll talk with him tonight and find
out what George wanted.

                    EMILY
I wouldn't trust George with a
newspaper after the dog had done her
business on them. I think he sees
turning good stuff bad as a game.
It's the only one he's good at.

                    RITA
               (Looks to her ringing
               phone)
Oh! It's that interview! It's this
afternoon! Can you cover for me?


                    EMILY
Only if you agree to let me land
with you two when I bail out of this
jerkwater town.


                    RITA
Emily! It's not that bad.


                    EMILY
Maybe not to you, but I think this
place is inbred, self-important and
moving in the wrong direction. I'd
like to put some miles between me
and my family … and George … and
some of those idiots we went to
school with.


                    RITA
Well, if you want me to move along
then you'll have to cover part of my
shift so I can go see the recruiter.
And in case he asks, just where do
you want us to move?


                    EMILY
Am I that obvious?


          -- END OF ACT II --

## **ACT III**
## **Scene 1**

Setting:  JOE and RITA are in the
Apartment Set, cuddled in
bed asleep.

GEORGE and EXTRAS sit at
tables in the Coffee Shop,
drinking coffee, looking
at computers, etc. The
actors move slowly. There
is no talking and nothing
should be done to attract
attention to this area of
the stage.

At Rise:  Apartment Set Lights Up.

JOE awakens from a
nightmare; thrashing around
it bed.

JOE (Moaning, yelling)
<u>No! … Not there! … To your right! …
Those wires there! … IED! … Six more
behind that building! … Watch out! …
Goddamn it!</u>

RITA
Joe, baby, it's OK. You're here at
home. With me. In our home. Let me
hold you. You're safe.
(RITA holds JOE)
It's OK, baby. It's OK

                    JOE
Christ!
                    (Sits up in bed)
Jeeze, Rita, will these dreams ever
end?


                    RITA
Someday they will. The VA folks told
me so.


                    JOE
                    (Gets out of bed, walks
                    about set.)
Crap! I got so wound up talking with
Chase and George that I forgot to go
see them yesterday. I'll do it
today. Promise. Sick call is at 10.


                    RITA
                    (Gets out of bed and moves
                    close enough to touch JOE
                    again.)
I'm glad to hear that. I worry about
you and those dreams.


                    JOE
I'd worry about me, too.
                    (Paces room)
You ought to be on this side of it.
I can see the Haj, smell them
                    (Scared and angry)
… and the fucking the desert. Rita …
the heat … I smell the heat.


                    RITA
I know baby. That's what you're
crying out about.

                    JOE
I know. I fucking well know that I'm
crying without tears. They told me
it would happen. I didn't believe
it.

                    RITA
The rules of PTSD don't change
because you want them to. Don't hold
it in. You can't cry without tears.

                    JOE
You don't know!

                    RITA
I know I don't. I'm not pretending
to. All I know is the symptoms they
told us to look for. I'm seeing
everything they said I would with
PTSD. That's why I'm glad you're
going to go see the VA today.

                    JOE
Yeah. I need to.
          (Beat)
That and tell Chase I'll take his
job.

                    RITA
You are! That's great! When did you
decide that?

                    JOE
Yesterday, really. I just wasn't
sure about it until now.

                    (JOE Continued)
I've got to find something to do
besides go to the Legion Hall and
drink.
                    (Beat)
Let George do that. We both know how
much I want to be like <u>him</u>.


                    RITA
George and Emily were together for a
while. Then he did something bad.
Bad enough that she won't talk
about, even to me! She told me he's
a real bastard.


                    JOE
There's something with him that I
can't put my finger on. He's telling
war stories and more than just
embellishing. I think he's told
folks he was in combat, which I know
he wasn't. He seems to have
convinced Roger and Bill he was.


                    RITA
Well, leopards don't often change
their spots. Remember, he lied to
everyone about you and the football
coach back in high school. And, he
lied about me screwing him before
you and I started dating.


                    JOE
I remember him telling me you were
good in bed.

                    RITA
What! You never told me he said
that!

                    JOE
That's 'cause I knew it was a lie.
          (Returns to Rita and holds
          her lovingly.)
I knew it was a lie because you're
not just good in bed … you're great
in bed.


                    RITA
Oh, Joe. You say those things!

          (JOE and RITA kiss
          passionately)

                    RITA
No time for that now, baby. I'm
supposed to meet that recruiter
again this morning. And, you need to
talk to the VA and Chase.

                    JOE
What are you going to tell the guy?

                    RITA
Yesterday afternoon he said he was
going to run my resume past hiring
officials at branches all over the
country. He wants me to come talk
with him at 9:30. I think this is
the payoff meeting … when they'll
talk positions, locations and money.
What time is it?

                    JOE
It's 8:15. You better get going.

                    RITA
          (Pats JOE on the bottom)
We ought to get going.

          (Exit JOE and RITA.)

          (Apartment Set Lights Dim)

          (Coffee Shop Lights Up)

                    GEORGE
          (Smiling deviously)
Let me see how things are this
morning
          (Beat)
Roger has Joe calling Chase an easy-
to-manipulate moron.
          (Beat)
And he's told everyone about Rita's
expertise with her hands and mouth.
Haw! He ought to know … that's an
area in his wheelhouse.
          (Beat)
Oh, that might be a bit over the
top! Let me add some emoticons
there!
          (Taps keyboard)
And here we have Bill playing Rita …
telling me we have to put our
relationship on hold for a while
because Joe is angry about it.
          (Beat)
Delicious! Let me add a bit to that.

(GEORGE Continued)

(Types keyboard while
speaking in a falsetto.)
Oh, George, it might be weeks before
I can have you again. I love you
sooooo much.
(Beat - Speaks in normal
voice)
Let me see … how about a message to
the plant's Production VP from a
headhunter quoting the Wall Street
Journal saying that combat vets are
causing liability problems on
factory floors across America.
(Beat)
And now … a bogus email from phony
Rita to the real Chase forwarding
the phony Joe message about Chase
being a moron? Oh, that's good!
(Taps keyboard)
And then another email from phony
Rita apologizing for that last one
and asking, no begging, 'Oh, Chase
please, please, please do not to
open that earlier email.'  That
should guarantee he opens it right
away!
(Taps keyboard)
Next up … an email to the Plant's HR
VP quoting a Wall Street Journal
article about deranged combat vets.
Today is the day that sleeping with
that skank pays off.
(Taps keyboard)

(GEORGE Continued)
And, for good measure, another one
suggesting that giving a hiring
preference to combat vets might be
grounds for a lawsuit by non-combat
vets.
            (Beat)
That ought to lower the good old
boy's job prospects a bit.
            (Beat)
Yes, that should do it. Since back
in high school Joe has had the
better of me and now it is time for
him to be history. And if they say I
manipulated Roger and Bill … those
drones … well, who would say it …
and who cares if they do?
            (Beat)
Maybe Bill and Roger? I saw doing
the nasty back then and now they
will dance to my tune  … HA! … And
they don't dare tell anyone or their
story will be read from coast to
coast. Technology makes it so simple
and easy to give it to them that
deserve it. And, all of them deserve
it.

            (Enter JOE and RITA - move
            from the Apartment Set
            into the Street Scene.)


                RITA
Joe! Don't look! There's George in
the Coffee Shop … again.

                    JOE
Where?

                    RITA
Don't look! He's over there, in the
window … working on a computer.

                    JOE
Oh, yeah. I see him.


                  GEORGE
(Smiles and waves at JOE and RITA)

                    RITA
Oh, crap, he saw us. He's waving.
His smile gives me the creeps.

                        (RITA and JOE wave at
                        GEORGE, then continue
                        walking across the stage.)

                    RITA
Joe, I've got to get to campus and
meet that recruiter. I'll text you
if it comes to anything. Cross you
fingers.

                    JOE
Will do. I'm off to see Chase. I'll
call if he has any good words. Bye

                        (RITA and JOE embrace.
                        They kiss.)

                    RITA
Bye, babe. See you tonight.

(Exit JOE and RITA)

GEORGE

Good old Joe. Such an easy mark. He believes in Rita and everything she says. Totally. Completely. My plan will work that faith against him.
(Beat)
He's going to be crossed and double-crossed and triple-crossed by those two ignorant fags. Then Joe, bless his trusting little heart, will see these email threads and believe his eyes not his mind. He can be led so easily to think Rita is cheating because he will trust what he thinks are her words.
(Beat)
Fools! These idiots have so little understanding of the world beyond appearances. Joe is just like Chase and the VP's at the plant. Simple people trusting that appearances are reality. Simple people unwilling to challenge appearances when those appearances make events seem clear and their lives seem easier.
(Beat)
God but I'd love to be a fly on the wall when Joe meets Chase today. Joe will shoot first rather than taking time to ask questions.
(Beat)

(GEORGE Continued)
Joe's opportunities in this town
will die when those emails I sent
out land in their intended inboxes.
We will see this end, with Rita and
Joe gone from town or separated … or
maybe both. It is delicious!
                    (Beat)
I may be judged guilty of meddling
by some … but who really cares. All
these fools will fear crossing me
after this. If they ever figure out
how stupidly they acted. And there's
little chance of <u>that</u>!
                    (Laughs)
Now, done. Time for a celebratory
beer.


          (Exit GEORGE)

          (Coffee Shop Lights Dim)

          (Street Scene Lights Dim)

## ACT III
## Scene 2

Setting:     GEORGE sits at a table in
             the dimly lit America
             Legion Bar. There is no
             talking and nothing should
             be done to attract
             attention this area of the
             stage.

             CHASE is in the HR Office.
             JESSICA sits on a chair or
             stands outside CHASE's HR
             Office. JESSICA is using
             her phone to send and
             receive text messages or
             browsing the web.

At Rise:     JOE Enters, and comes to
             the office door.


                    JESSICA
Joe! I heard you were back in town.
Welcome home.

                      JOE
Jessica? I haven't seen you in God
knows how long. Are you waiting to
see Chase, too?

                    JESSICA
Yeah, I'm early.

                    JOE
I'm a bit early myself.
          (Knocks on door.)

                  CHASE
Joe, you're early! Good to see you.
Come on in. Have a chair.
          (To JESSICA)
You're next, Jessica. Make yourself
comfortable.
          (Closes door. Speaks to
          JOE)
Can I get you a cup of coffee?

                    JOE
Sure.

                  CHASE
          (Gets JOE a cup of coffee)
Here, Joe for Joe.

                    JOE
Thanks. I've thought about our
conversation yesterday. That
Assistant Office Manager opportunity
intrigues me. If the position is
still open I'd like to take you up
on your offer.

                  CHASE
Great! I'll slide your name into
that slot. Here is a new-employee
packet for you to look at as.
          (Hands a packet to Joe.
          Sits and taps on computer.
Huh? What the hell?

                              JOE
          What's up?


                             CHASE
          I don't know what the shit's going
          on. All the positions I'm filling
          say they have been closed. They were
          open when I came in this morning.
          It's probably some computer glitch.
          Let me go check it out.
                         (CHASE leaves his office.
                         He passes Jessica waiting
                         outside the door.)
          Oh! Jessica, I'll be about ten
          minutes late. There's been some
          computer problem. If you can wait
          I'll be right back.


                           JESSICA
                         (Quietly)
          OK.


                         (Exit CHASE)


                           JESSICA
                         (Checking her phone)
          That's odd.
                         (Beat)
          That, too.


                         (Enter CHASE)


                            CHASE
          Thanks for waiting, Jessica.
                         (Goes into office.)
          Joe. I'm not sure what's going on.
          My VP closed all the positions I've

                    (CHASE Continued)
been filling. That, and she'll set
up a meeting for me right before
lunch.
                    (Beat)
If I didn't know better, Joe, I
think she's getting ready to fire
me, or some such shit.

                    JOE
                    (Stands angrily. Badly
                    surprised.)
Come on Chase! George told me you'd
pull the rug out from me. <u>Goddamn
it</u>! I hate that you've proved him
right.

                    (Exit JOE - Stomps out of
                    Office and past JESSICA)

                    CHASE
                    (Calls to JOE as he
                    exits.)
<u>Joe! Wait! I'll call you later!</u>
                    (Dejected)
As soon as I find out what the
hell's going on here!

                    JESSICA
What's with Joe?

                    CHASE
Wish I could tell you Jessica, but I
really don't know what's going on.
Come in and grab a chair.

> (CHASE and JESSICA go into
> the office. JESSICA sits.
> CHASE shuts the door and
> moves behind his desk.)

CHASE

Jessica, your file shows you've made
good progress; enough that I've
decided that this is the last
meeting we need to have. I'm going
to certify you're again qualified to
work the shop floor again.
> (Beat)
Congratulations.

JESSICA

Thank you! It's been a tough couple
of months. I have to admit I'm
exhausted. Chase, we've known each
other since middle school. You know
me as well as anyone. You have to
know that I could not have pulled
myself out of this without your
help. And the next few months are
going to be challenging.
> (JESSICA pats her stomach
> - she is pregnant but has
> not told anyone)

CHASE

Don't embarrass me. I'm not so sure
about that. You've always been a
strong woman, Jessica. I wish you
knew that. You don't need someone to
lean on for the day-to-day stuff.
Stay away from that crap and stick
with your 12-step programs when

(CHASE Continued)
you're feeling down. OK?

                    JESSICA
Someday I will be OK. Believe me
when I tell you you've done more for
me than you know, Chase! You help
people. You're a good man and I
appreciate it.
          (Pause. Looks at the door)
You know Joe better than me. I'm not
sure what happened with Joe just
now. But something doesn't look
right.

                    CHASE
That's just some personnel stuff I
can't discuss. But, some weird stuff
happened this morning and he's
pissed at me. You and him were close
for a while back in school, weren't
you? Does he seem changed to you?

                    JESSICA
Yes … yes we were close. But all
that ended when Joe hooked up with
Rita. And … well … he's as dedicated
to her now as he was back then. And
her to him, too. The whole town
knows that. You saw how he blew by
me out the hallway. I'm not sure he
knows I exist now, at least not in a
personal sense.
          (Beat)
That's what makes some Facebook
stuff I just saw so weird.

                    CHASE
What stuff?


                    JESSICA
Here …  Stuff that just doesn't look
right. Check it out on my phone.
          (Hands phone to CHASE)
It looks like Joe's making passes at
me … but that's just not so … I mean
… the hallway just now. I'd know if
we were flirting. I guarantee you we
are not. But … well it looks to me
like someone is spoofing him. Look
at Rita's page. It looks like she's
just ending an affair with George,
and <u>you</u>. And even I know that's
bullshit.


                    CHASE
What! How? If you don't mind me
asking.


                    JESSICA
Well, George and I have an … an …
arrangement. We hooked up when he
got back into town last year. When
he's lonely he calls me. And vice-
versa.
          (Points to stomach)
This child is his.

I know this is out of your area. But
we both know Joe and Rita.
And we both know this sort of crap
isn't like them. Between you and me
it looks more like old George's
handiwork.

(JESSICA Continued)
That guy we both knew and hated back
in high school. He always was one to
throw hand grenades just for the fun
of watching the explosions.

CHASE
You know more than you're saying.
Spill it.

JESSICA
That falls under the heading of
pillow talk. The boy talks in his
sleep.
(Beat)
I know you and Joe have been best
friends since school. I know you and
Joanne are matched like peas in a
pod. I know both of you like Joe and
Rita. All four of you are really
good people.
(Beat)
You might want to do some digging
and see what's really what and who's
really who out there.

CHASE
Thanks for the pointer.
(Hands JESSICA her phone)
Now, like I said earlier. You're
cleared to head back to your job on
the shop floor.

(CHASE Continued)
I don't ever want to see you up here
again at least for this kind of
stuff anyway.

                    JESSICA
You won't. Thanks again, Chase. I'd
kiss you but I like Joanne too much.
Tell her hello for me.

                    CHASE
I will. Good-bye, now. And thanks
for the tip about that on-line
stuff.
                    (Chase stands, so does
                    Jessica, they shake hands)

          (Exit JESSICA)

                    CHASE
                    (Picks up phone and dials)
Sam, this is Chase up in HR. Like I
mentioned yesterday, Jessica is
cleared to work the shop floor
again. She's headed back your way
now.
Yeah, light duty if you can. She's
pregnant and that has to be part of
her job responsibilities.
                    (Pause, listening)
Keep me informed if there are any
more performance problems. Bye.
                    (Hangs up phone and looks
                    at computer)
Now, what the hell is going on?

                    (HR Office Lights Dim.
                    CHASE continues working
                    and EXITS discreetly after
                    action shifts to the
                    American Legion Bar)

(American Legion Bar
Lights Up)

JOE

Well, George, I hate to tell you how
right you were. Chase just pulled
the rug out from under me. All those
positions he was promising have
magically closed.
(Beat)
What a screw job. I guess you and I
are in the same club now.

GEORGE

(Raising his glass)
Welcome to another member of the
screwed-over-by-Chase club.
(Calls to bartender)
A tall, cold one for my friend here!

(BARTENDER brings beers to
GEORGE and JOE)

GEORGE

Joe, good buddy, I raise my glass to
you. You're a far better man than
most anyone else in this town. Hell,
you're better than this town, let
alone the people in it.

JOE

Back at you. From what you said
yesterday, I figured you've had some
issues with Chase, too.

                    GEORGE
Yeah, I have. To be honest, the guy
just doesn't like me. Never has.
About six months ago I had an
interview with the plant manager and
I think Chase must have called the
guy and put the blackball on me.
Nothing I could say seemed to hit
the mark; no answer I gave to a
question was good enough. It was
like the first day in Basic
Training.

                    JOE
I know what you mean. At least you
got to talk with the manager. Chase
gave me a line about the positions
having been closed this morning. He
even said it looks like his boss is
going to fire him.

                    GEORGE
That's a load of crap. He's the guy
who keeps their HR unit in
compliance with the federal rules.
If the positions ever <u>were</u> opened
he'd be the one to close them.
          (Beat)
Face it, Joe. Chase has fucked us
both real good. The question is ...
what are you going to do about it?

                    JOE
I don't know right yet. What I do
know is that a couple more of this
is needed. Bartender! Two more of
these.

                    GEORGE
Thanks, man. Thanks a bunch.
          (Beat)
Chase has always manipulated people.
Remember all that crap with the
Coach back in high school. It took
me until three months ago to learn
that Chase set all that in motion.

               (Enter BILL, comes to
               where JOE and GEORGE sit)

                    GEORGE
It must be quitting time. Here comes
Bill.

                    BILL
Got room for another one there?

                    JOE
Sure do.
          (Waves and calls to
          BARTENDER.)
Make that another one, too. Better
yet, bring us the bottle!

                    BILL
Thanks, Joe. What's the occasion?

                    GEORGE
Chase just screwed Joe. Seems he was
guaranteed a management position at
the plant. But this morning Chase
told him it suddenly closed. You
know anything about it?

                    BILL
Only that my boss told this morning
to wear a dress shirt and tie
tomorrow so I can talk with the
floor manager about a promotion.

          (BARTENDER puts bottle in
          front of JOE)

                    JOE
          (Pours himself a drink)
But that is one of the positions
Chase told me closed!

                    BILL
Well … somebody is lying because I
have a 10 AM appointment tomorrow.
Take a look.
          (Passes a paper to JOE)
See, this was in my plant mailbox
this morning. Shirt and tie
specifically mentioned.

                    JOE
          (Finishes his drink and
          fills glass again)
Fuck!

          (GEORGE and BILL exchange
          looks behind JOE'S back)

                    GEORGE
Joe, I hate to be the bearer of bad
news. But some of your problems
might be of a more domestic nature.

                    JOE
What!


                    BILL
Do you check your social media pages
often?


                    JOE
No. When I was overseas it was too
damn depressing. Don't do it now,
either.


                    BILL
You haven't checked Rita's pages in
a while?


                    JOE
She told me she didn't have time for
that kind of crap.


                    BILL
          (Lays a phone on the bar)
Well, buddy ... looks like you ought
to make time now.


               (JOE looks at the phone.
               Flips through a few pages.
               Angrily stands up and
               looks at GEORGE.)


                    JOE
What the hell! You and Rita! Chase
and Rita! Bill and Rita! What the
hell! She's sleeping with the whole
fucking town!

GEORGE

Joe, if you see anything in there about me and Rita you gotta' understand one thing. She started it, not me. It was while you were over in the sandbox the second time. Maybe she got lonely. Man, I'm sorry. She told me the two of you were done. I thought she just wanted to talk. Be mad at her … not jealous of me.

JOE
(Finishes drink in one swallow.)

What the fuck! <u>Stand up you Goddamn asshole!</u>

(GEORGE stands)

(JOE hits GEORGE)

(GEORGE falls to floor)

JOE

You fucking little asshole! You're the same little jerk you've always been. You better say the hell out of my way or I'll kick the living shit out of you. If I see your slimy face I'll fucking break you in half.

(JOE takes bottle and storms out of the bar and onto Street Scene)

                    BARTENDER
You want me to call the Police?

                    GEORGE
               (Amused)
No way man. No way.
               (Beat)
Well played, Bill. Well played. Now,
let's raise some beer our friend's
bad luck.

                    (GEORGE rubs his jaw for
                    effect as he and BILL
                    laugh)

                    (American Legion Bar
                    Lights Dim)

                    (Street Scene Lights Up)

                    (JOE paces the Street
                    Scene, looking at a phone
                    and occasionally drinking
                    from a bottle. He is very
                    angry, now is drunk, and
                    is getting drunker.)

                    JOE
Stupid! Stupid! Stupid! How could I
have been so Goddamn stupid?
               (Beat)
I'm over there lonely as hell and
she's getting lonely back here. I'm
getting my ass shot at and she's
giving shots of ass and more.
               (Beat)

(JOE Continued)

And going to George! George! Of all the fucking people in this fucking town … why the hell did she sleep with him? And Bill and Roger, too! Those two zits for brains!

(Beat)

And Chase! My best buddy. Best! Best! Best … my ass. Chase taking her, too.

(Beat)

The Army told us to watch out for this. But I didn't think she'd do it. She's nothing more than a cheating, cheap-ass-whore.

(Beat)

A whore I love … loved … wanted to love. Wanted to love so much I was blind to her whoring. That's her, nothing more than a common whore.

(Beat)

She blindfolded me with words of love while she whored all over town.

(Beat)

And it took jerks like Bill and George to pull my blindfold off. Who'd of thought it would be those two losers who helped me. My only friends are those I thought were losers. What does that make me?

(Beat)

Guess that makes me a loser, too. A well-fucked-over loser. A loser in loser-town. A loser who thought his wife's lover was his best friend. A loser who thought the friend was a loser is the real loser.

(JOE Continued)
>           (Beat)
George says I should be mad at her,
not jealous of him. Why not? Because
it's him that's telling the truth.
That's why!
>           (Beat)
She … she … Rita-the-whore … now she
is the one I am angry with. The
lying bitch-whore!
>           (Beat)
And Chase!
>           (Beat)
The bastard sings the whore's
praises while having a shot of her
on the sly. He tells me again and
again, 'She only has eyes for you.'
If that is true it is because she
had her eyes closed while he drilled
her in bed! And in MY bed, too …
Jesus-fucking-Christ … In my own
bed, too!
>           (Beat)
These pages … these pages … it's all
there in their own words … for all
the world to see … their love? … No!
There is no love here. There is only
lust and betrayal and faithlessness
and whoredom!
>           (Beat)
The ones I trusted are liars and the
ones I thought were liars are
truthful. What has become of this
world?
>           (Beat)

(JOE Continued)
I'll send George a message and
apologize for hitting him. Maybe he
knows more than he said.
(Taps on phone)
Ah! George says he is sorry. A
thousand times sorry. He wants to be
my friend. I should dump Rita and
Chase. Yes … dump them … leave them
with their affairs. Yes. Get out of
this town and leave them all to
their own small selves!
(Beat)
I'll go back to the Army. Yes!
That's what I'll do. Let me go pack
my shit and get the hell out of this
shit-hole of a town.

(Exit JOE - towards
Apartment Set)

## ACT III
## Scene 3

Setting:  CHASE is in the HR Office
working on his computer.
Initially, the lights are
dim. He is moving slowly
so as not to attract
audience attention.

RITA and EMILY are working
in the Diner.

At Rise:  RITA and EMILY come to the
front of the Diner


                    EMILY
So, are you going to take the job or
not?

                    RITA
I have until tomorrow to give him my
answer. If I had to decide right now
I would. I'd say 'Yes' just to get
me and Joe out of this town.

                    EMILY
Have you told him yet?

                    RITA
No, he's not answering his phone. He
was supposed to meet Chase earlier.
          (Beat)
Let me call and see if he knows
where Joe's gone.

                    (RITA Continued)

                    (Enters numbers on phone)
          Chase? It's Rita. Have you seen or
          heard from Joe this afternoon?

                    (Lights up in CHASE's
                    Office)

                         CHASE
          Rita! No. There was a problem with
          those open positions this morning.
          Joe thought I was blowing him off.
          He left here very angry. I've got it
          straightened out on this end, but
          there is another problem.
                    (Beat)
          I was just about to call you.
          Someone is posting a bunch of crap
          about all of us on social media. I
          asked our IT security guy to figure
          it out for me. He just called me
          saying it looks like someone has set
          up phony social media pages for you
          and me, and Joe, too. Whoever did it
          is has posted some weird shit Rita.

                         RITA
          What kind of weird?

                         CHASE
          They're making it out that you had a
          string of affairs while Joe was out
          of the country.

                    RITA
Who would they do that? I don't use
social media … neither does Joe. Who
is saying those things?

                    CHASE
I don't know who it is, but someone
is screwing with the three of us.
I'm going to send you an email with
the links. And, Rita, don't be
upset. Go to your happy place before
you read them. They're a bunch of
crap. I only hope Joe hasn't seen
them yet.

                    RITA
That bad?

                    CHASE
Worse than bad. They're saying
you've been sleeping with George and
Bill and Roger and me … and a bunch
of others, too … half the county.

                    RITA
Oh my God!

                    CHASE
Rita … Rita… I just received another
email from my security guy. I'm
sending you the links now. Take a
look at them and call me back.

                    (CHASE hangs up and goes
                    back to working on his
                    computer.)

                    RITA
              (Taps keys on phone)
Oh my God, Emily. Look at this.
Someone is saying I've been sleeping
with George and Chase. And … look.

              (RITA cries and hands
              phone to EMILY)

                    EMILY
Who would do that? Who would believe
it?
              (Pause while looking)
Joe! Someone is trying to get to Joe
and you!
              (Beat)
The only person I know who fits that
description would be George. But
this is too much even for him.
              (Beat)
At least I think it is too much for
him.
              (Pause while looking at
              pages)
What! This date! When you were
supposed to be with him. The bastard
was with me out in California!

              (RITA'S phone rings)

                    RITA
              (Looks at phone)
It's Chase!
              (Answers phone)
Chase! My God! What is going on?

                         CHASE
The security folks tell me the
posting come from three distinct
users. Our good-old-pal George is
one. The other two are accounts
created by George but being updated
by Roger and Bill.
                  (Beat)
It makes sense to me. Those two were
up for promotions into the jobs Joe
interviewed for. I think these two
are trying to poison the environment
here at the plant for Joe and guys
like him.


                         RITA
But how? Why? Those two are idiots
but they can't be that stupid!


                         CHASE
Maybe they are and maybe they're
not. George might be behind it all.
Security has an email he sent to VPs
claiming to be a headhunter passing
along a report from the Wall Street
Journal saying that combat vets were
bad supervisors because of PTSD.
                  (Beat)
And he followed that up with another
one suggesting that giving a hiring
preference to combat vets was
illegal.


                         RITA
That didn't work … did it?

                    CHASE
It did for about an hour. The VP had
the factory floor manager reset
interviews with Bill and Roger for
tomorrow. I got that straightened
out late this afternoon and those
interviews have been cancelled. The
shit is squarely in the fan about
this.

                    RITA
Have you told Joe?

                    CHASE
Not yet. I've set him a couple of
messages asking him to call me but
he hasn't answered.

                    RITA
He's not answering me either. I'm
going to go home and see if he's
there.
            (Hangs up phone.)
Emily! It looks like George, Bill
and Roger fabricated this because
they were cut out of promotions at
the plant.

                    EMILY
Isn't Bill your cousin?

                    RITA
Yeah. He always had a perverted
sense that he needs to protect me
from Joe for some reason. I'll kill
him when I see him.

                    EMILY
Get home! Find Joe and straighten
him out. I'll cover here for you.

                    RITA
Ok! Thanks.

                    EMILY
And call me when you get there.

                    RITA
Thanks. I will. If you talk to Joe
tell him I'm at home waiting for
him. Tell him I have to talk with
him.

          (Exit RITA)

                    EMILY
          (Takes phone and taps
          keys)
None of these dates match up. George
couldn't have been screwing Rita
then!

          (Enter GEORGE and JESSICA)

          (GEORGE is holding JESSICA
          by the arm, more pulling
          than walking with her.)

                    GEORGE
          (Talking as they enter.)
… next week I'll bet. Then things
between you and him will get back on
track.
          (Looks at EMILY)

(GEORGE Continued)
Hey beautiful, some coffee for us.

EMILY
George, you slimy son of a bitch!
What are you trying to do to Rita
and Joe?

GEORGE
Emily, Emily, Emily … you and
Jessica here have finally discovered
that Joe is back in town and
searching for a new girlfriend. I
was just telling Jessica that she
and Joe ought to hook up. It would
be good for both of them.

EMILY
Get your lying, sack of shit ass out
of here before I call the cops!

GEORGE
Sure thing, beautiful. Whatever you
say. Just remember me when you feel
those needs and wants and it's late
at night.

EMILY
That will be a cold day in hell. Get
out of here before I throw something
at you.

GEORGE
And, ladies, if I were you I'd watch
out for Roger and Joe.

(GEORGE Continued)
They've been hitting the sauce a
bit. As angry as they are it would
be a shame to get in their way.

(Exit GEORGE - Laughing)

EMILY
Good to see his ass going away!
(Studies Jessica)
My excuse is that I started sleeping
with him before learning how big an
asshole he is. What's yours?

JESSICA
I'm dealing with that now. Emily,
what George said about Rita and Joe
… he's been gloating about breaking
them up and hooking me up with Joe.
It's all a game to him.
(Beat)
Everyone in town knows I've always
liked Joe, but what George is saying
just doesn't make any sense to me.
Are he and Rita having problems or
is George just stirring the pot? He
does that for fun, you know.

EMILY
I know him and it sounds like you're
getting to know him well enough now,
too, Jessica,
(Beat)
You need to stay away from Joe and
Rita … at least for the time being.

(EMILY Continued)
From what I've heard George has been
working with a couple of others to
screw Joe out of a job and break up
their relationship. Who's he's been
seeing lately?

JESSICA
He tries to keep me away from my
friends, but I know sees a lot of
people, mostly down at the Legion
Hall.
            (Beat)
I've heard rumors that he's been
keeping time with a muckity-muck
lady from down at the plant. That
pisses me off when I think it. What
hurts worse is when I've complained
to him about it he laughs it off …
saying since I don't know the skanks
that makes it OK. Like sleeping with
them that way isn't spitting on me.

EMILY
What about those two guys we went to
school with, Bill and Roger?

JESSICA
I've heard him say those names in
his sleep. Last night he was
laughing after a few drinks. Saying
things that didn't make any sense.
"Roger as Rita … Billy as Joe … Me
in between." He was drunk and I
thought he was talking about
drinking margaritas and listening to
Billy Joel.

                    EMILY
What happened with Chase this
afternoon?

                    JESSICA
I had a meeting with Chase … at the
plant … some HR stuff. Joe was there
before me and they had a hell of an
argument. Joe accused Chase of lying
to him and nearly knocked me on my
ass as he stomped out.
          (Beat)
I know those two guys … they were
best friends. Now, with George
talking shit about them, it makes me
wonder just what the hell he's at.

          (EMILY'S Phone rings, she
          answers)

                    EMILY
Chase! What's up?

                    CHASE
Its all George's doing. I just gave
the details to Rita.

                    EMILY
She was here when you called and I
overheard. That would be typical for
that slime-ball. He brought Jessica
here just after you called Rita. The
asshole is as cock sure as he's ever
been. I looked at those web postings
and there're a bunch of flat-out
lies.

(EMILY Continued)

One of the dates George claims to
have been banging Rita he was
banging me out in California. And I
can prove it. The worm left me to
pay the damn room bill. That's why I
kicked his sorry ass out.

                    JESSICA
               (So CHASE can hear)
I'm sure Bill and Roger are in on
this, too. Those weird posts sound
like a game George is playing … you
know, pitting Joe against Rita.
Roger sounds almost as much like
Rita as Rita herself, but Bill isn't
angry enough to be Joe!

                    CHASE
I'm going to expose the bastard with
some postings of my own!

                    EMILY
Didn't you hear what Jessica said?
I'm not sure I'd do that. You're
playing with fire. Rita has gone
home to talk with Joe and I'm
worried about her.

                    CHASE
Let me come down there and we can go
over to their place and straighten
this out.

                    EMILY
OK. See you here. *Shit!*

(EMILY pockets phone)

JESSICA

Emily, I hate to ask right now but
can you do me a favor? I don't want
to stay with George tonight. I think
he suspects I'm pregnant and the way
he's acting is beginning to scare
me. Could you give me a ride out to
my folk's house out on Upper River
Road? I know it's a long ways out.
But I'm really afraid of staying
with him now.

EMILY

OK. Let's get going.
        (Yells to off-stage)
Fred! I've got to run an errand.
I'll be back in an hour. The counter
is yours until then!
        (Beat)
I haven't shared this with anyone,
but the reason I dumped George was
he started acting like me not
wanting to having children with him
was a personal affront to his
character.

JESSICA

I know what you mean. That's why I
think he's found out I'm pregnant.
For the last two months he's been
acting differently. He's keeping
tabs on me and watching my phone
calls. It's like I'm a pet or a toy.

(JESSICA Continued)
Not his lover or friend or even
roommate.

It's like he thinks he owns me now.
I'm frightened of what he might do.

EMILY
That sounds like what he tried to do
with me. I caught him trashing my
birth control pills when we were on
a trip out in California. I think
the boy sees fatherhood as proving
manhood and he wants someone,
anyone, to give him a child. It
scares me to think what he'd do
then.
(Beat)
You've got to stay away from him.
(Beat)
We can talk on the way out to your
folks.

(Exit EMILY and JESSICA)

CHASE
(Discovers something on
his computer screen)
Jesus Christ!
(Picks up phone and dials)

Come on Emily! Answer your phone! Be
there!
(Beat)
Voicemail … crap!
(Beat)

(CHASE Continued)
Emily, I wanted to touch base with
you about some more information I've
found out. I'm on my way down there
now. If you get this call me.
Otherwise I'll see you at the
restaurant.

## ACT III
## Scene 4

Setting:   GEORGE sits in the
           American Legion Bar
           drinking and fiddling with
           his smartphone.

           RITA sits waiting for JOE.
           In the he Apartment Set,
           which is half-lit. Nothing
           should be done to distract
           attention from the action
           in the American Legion Bar
           or Street Scene.

At Rise:   ROGER enters the American
           Legion Bar.


           (Enter ROGER)

                    ROGER
George! How're they hangin'?

                    GEORGE
Comfortably, my good man, quite
comfortably. Have a sit-down. I've
got something to show you.
           (Shows ROGER his phone)
You might want to take a shot of
courage while you look at what's up
with our little game.

                    (GEORGE Hands ROGER a
                    glass of whiskey)

(GEORGE Continued)
Looks like you've done a good job.
Maybe a bit too good. Chase is
posting shit like this all over the
place. He's calling you a fine hunk
of woman.

ROGER
(Empties glass in in one
swig)
What's that fag know about it?
Jeeze. What else is he saying about
me, I mean Rita?

GEORGE
(Reading screen)
Well, Chase claims to know it is
you, specifically, pretending to be
Rita. And he saying you're doing
such a good job of mimicking a woman
because you've a lot of experience
playing the girl side of a
relationship. He's outing you and
Bill for those days back in high
school.

ROGER
What the fuck!
(Beat)
How the hell did he find out I was
playing Rita? It was supposed to be
a secret between you and me.
(Empties glass in one
swig)
Bartender! … Give me another one of
these! No! Bring me the bottle.

                    GEORGE
              (Reading screen)
He goes on. Here he says that Bill
has been pretending to be Joe; and
that you're both stupid because
anyone with a shred of technical
ability could have hidden their
footprints better. Then there is
some text cut from log files showing
when you and Bill posted to the
site. He's nailed the two of you
pretty good.


                    ROGER
Bill? I thought it was just you and
me in on this one.


                    GEORGE
The game got bigger than I thought
it would. I needed both you and
Bill. People I could trust and Bill
fit right in. No matter - when we're
done with this game I'll pull the
profiles down and it all goes away.


              (BARTENDER puts bottle in
              front of ROGER)


                    ROGER
              (Empties glass in one
              swig)
Easy for you! You're not the one
being called a woman. Damn him.
All my friends will see this. And my
parents, too.
              (Beat)

(ROGER Continued)

I'm going to catch up with that bastard and teach him a lesson he won't be able to forget.

> (On the way out of the bar he picks up the bottle and drinks deeply)

> (Exit ROGER - Carrying a bottle to the Street Scene.)

GEORGE

(Taps phone)

That fool and his sweet nectar! I better tell Bill that Chase just dished some shit about our game. He needs to watch out for Roger tonight. The boy's got a bottle and is really pissed that Chase outed him. We both know how touchy he is about that subject.

> (To himself as he taps keyboard.)

It'll be better once this game is over and these fools think all these postings are deleted. Too bad neither of those dorks know that what's posted on-line stays online forever.

(Laughs)

(American Legion Bar Lights Dim)

(Street Scene Lights Up)

                    ROGER
               (Stumbling, drunk)
The man has no right, no fucking
right, telling secrets like that.
               (Beat)
What's a man to do when he knows his
family will disown him? You tell me
that mister HR manager. You tell me
that!
               (Taps leys on phone)
I tell you what a man does. He
fights back!
               (Pause while call is
               connected)
Chase, old buddy, old pal, old
friend. Nobody can treat me like
that. You fucking asshole!
               (Beat)
Not you! Not Joe! Not no fucking
body. Nobody!
               (Puts phone away and
               displays a handgun to the
               audience)
No fucking buddy!

               (Exit ROGER)

               (Street Scene Lights Dim)

               (Enter CHASE - Hastily
               enters the Diner and calls
               into the kitchen)

                    CHASE
Emily! Emily!

(Enter EMILY - not from
kitchen.)

CHASE

Oh God, there you are! I've been
texting and calling you!

EMILY
(Reaches behind counter
and produces phone.)
I was taking Jessica out to her
folks place out on River Road. I
forgot my phone. Besides, I already
got one $125 ticket! My next one is
$250 and I can't afford that.

CHASE

Have you seen Rita?

EMILY

Not since earlier when she went home
to find Joe. What's up?

CHASE

I blew the whistle on George, Bill
and Roger. I know you said I
shouldn't do it but I did. And then
George texted to me accidentally, at
least I think it was accidentally,
telling Bill to watch out for Roger.
Then Roger called me yelling and
screaming. He sounded drunk and
apparently wants to teach me a
lesson.

                    EMILY
Chase, I wouldn't count on that text
being an accident. George does a lot
of things just to stir up drama.

                    CHASE
What'd you ever see in the guy?

                    EMILY
There was a time when I wanted drama
in my life.
          (Checks phone)
You weren't joking about calling me.
Looks like you sent me four text
messages and five phone calls. Oh!
There's one from Rita, too.
          (Holds phone to ear.)
Shit! She says that Joe's and his
stuff are gone. Let me call her.
          (Presses some phone keys)

          (Lights up in Apartment
          Set)

                    RITA
          (Answering phone.)
Joe!?

                    EMILY
Rita, are you OK?

                    RITA
Oh! Emily … I'm OK. Joe got home
before me and packed his gear.
          (She cries)
He's gone. He won't answer my calls
or texts.

                    EMILY
Chase, Jessica and me figured out
what's going on. George set up Bill
and Roger to play you and Joe. We
think his goal was to split the two
of you up.

                    RITA
That's all? All this for that? Why

                    EMILY
Mostly just to stir up shit. You
know how that asshole works! Right
now, he's gloating because he thinks
he screwed Joe out of a job.
Totaling your relationship was just
collateral damage, a side benefit.
          (Beat)
Have you seen Roger or Bill? Chase
outed them and now he's concerned
they might be headed out to get even
with all of us.

                    RITA
Bill? He's my cousin! I've known him
my whole life. Everyone in the
family knows he's gay. He may talk a
lot but he won't do anything. Roger
… he's another story.

                    EMILY
Chase outed Roger, and he's drinking
and now is ranting at him on the
phone and all over the web.

                         RITA
Why? The half of town that doesn't
know Roger is gay probably doesn't
care one way or the other. And those
who do know he's gay probably won't
treat him any differently than they
do now. He's not the most social
person in the world.

                        EMILY
Well, watch out for him. Me and
Chase are headed your way now. We'll
look for Joe on the way over.

                         RITA
OK. If you see him tell him I love
him and that he shouldn't believe
all these lies.

                    (EMILY and RITA hang up
                     their phones)

                        EMILY
Chase, if you were trying to get out
of town where would you go besides
the bus station?

                        CHASE
At this time of night that would be
about it.


                        EMILY
Let's go.

                    (EMILY and CHASE move into
                     the Street Scene)

(Diner Lights Dim)

(Street Scene Lights Up)

(Enter JOE enters onto the
Street Scene. He is drunk
and carries a suitcase.
Stands furthest from
Diner.)

                    CHASE
Emily, I think you were right.
Calling Roger and Bill out was
stupid. I should have listened to
you.

                    EMILY
That's something you get to deal
with tomorrow at work.

                    CHASE
Yeah.
          (Points to JOE)
Isn't that Joe at the bus stop over
there?

                    (CHASE and EMILY cross the
                    Street Scene to where JOE
                    stands)

                    EMILY
Joe! Jeeze are we happy to find you.

                    JOE
Why? Want to beat up on the loser
some more?

                    CHASE
Buddy, you're wasted drunk! What do
you mean beat you up? I've been
trying to get through to you all
day. That situation here at the
plant has been cleared up. George
lied to the VP's and they believed
him for about an hour or so. They
figured it out and everything is set
up for you to interview tomorrow.

                    JOE
Bullshit, Chase! All this time I
thought you were my best friend. I
believed you. … I believed
everything you said. You fucking
liar! All the time you were setting
me up you were dicking my Rita. You
asshole!
                    (Throws bottle at Chase,
                    misses, then takes an
                    ineffective swing at him.)
I'm going back to the Army. Least
there folks didn't act like shits.

                    CHASE
Joe, you're too drunk be out here.
Let's get you home.

                    EMILY
Rita is waiting for you there. She
wants to talk with you about all
these lies. It's taken all day but
we figured out who's behind it all.

                    CHASE
Emily, I'm not sure he's ready for
that.

                    EMILY
You're probably right, Chase.
          (Beat)
Joe, let Chase and me get you home.

                    (Enter BILL and ROGER - on
                    far side of Street Scene
                    from Chase, Emily and Joe)

                    BILL
Look! Three of the dynamic foursome.

                    ROGER
          (Pulls out the handgun)
Fucking assholes!

                    (ROGER runs to where
                    CHASE, EMILY and JOE
                    stand. BILL is close
                    behind. CHASE moves so
                    EMILY and JOE are behind
                    him.)

                    ROGER
Chase! You … are … a … fucking …
asshole!

                    BILL
Roger, you're drunk? Put that gun
away!

                    ROGER
What? You're a fan of theirs now?

                    BILL
No. I'm just not a fan of getting
into fights with drunks. Like you
and Joe now.


                    ROGER
          (Aiming pistol at CHASE
Then go home little boy.


                    BILL
          (Blocks line of fire)
No, damn it Roger. You don't know
what you're doing. This was George's
game not yours ... not mine ... and
damn sure wasn't theirs.
          (Beat)
George is pissed at the world. He
has been since high school. You
should know that.
          (Beat)
It was George squealing to the Coach
about you and me that got him kicked
him off the football team! He's been
blaming everyone here except himself
for that. Right now he's probably
laughing at all of us.


                    ROGER
Bill, I love you but stand aside! No
matter what happened back then ...
          (Pointing pistol towards
          CHASE)
... that man there said things today
that shouldn't have been said.
          (Beat)
By anyone

                    BILL
             (Does not move)
Roger! Words can't kill.

                    CHASE
Let him go. The gay bastard doesn't
have the balls to shoot.

                    ROGER
Stand aside or die! Now, Bill!

                    BILL
             (Does not move.)

                    ROGER
             (For a moment seems to
             lower pistol in
             resignation - before
             firing it. The round hits
             BILL mid-torso.)

                    BILL
             (Falls to the ground
             clutching his mid-section)

                    ROGER
             (Seems stunned. Wavers.
             Then aims the pistol at
             his head and wavers again.
             Then fires a second round
             is into his head. Falls
             dead.)

                    EMILY
             (Screams - jumps into
             CHASE'S arms.)

                    JOE
          (Kicks weapon away from
          ROGER'S hand. He takes a
          knee looking at the
          bodies. Authoritative,
          experienced reactions.)
Bill's probably still alive! This
one's toast! Call a medic!
          (Picks up pistol and tucks
          it away.)
This may come in handy!


          (Exit JOE - towards
          Apartment Set)

                    EMILY
          (Calling 911)
Oh, God. Oh, God. Chase! What
happened?


                    CHASE
Damn. I really didn't think he had
it in him. Fuck!


          (Enter OFFICER - Kneels by
          BILL and ROGER)

                    OFFICER
I heard shots! What happened?
          (Into radio)
Shots Fired! Two down with gunshots!
          (To Emily and Chase)
What happened?

                    EMILY
He … shot Bill then himself.

                    OFFICER
Where's the weapon, Ma'am? If he
shot them there ought to be a
weapon?

                     CHASE
Oh my God! Joe took it. Oh God! We
have to stop him. He's drunk and
gone to kill Rita!

                    OFFICER
Who? Where?

                     EMILY
I can take you there!

                    OFFICER
               (To CHASE)
You stay here. Don't let anybody
touch anything.
               (Beat)
If someone needs me call 911. Have
dispatch put them through to me.
I'll be on the radio.
               (To EMILY)
Let's go ma'am. Fill me in on the
way.

          (Exit EMILY and OFFICER)

          (Apartment Set Lights Up.)

          (Enter JOE into the
          Apartment Set)

                    JOE
    Time to deal with her.
            (Bangs on locked door,
            yelling)
    Rita! God damn it, Rita! Open this
    door.

                    RITA
            (Opens door)
    Joe. Babe, what's wrong?

                    JOE
            (Pushes RITA away)
    You damn sure know what's wrong. I
    found out you've been screwing half
    the men in town. I'm off fighting
    the war and you're in bed with every
    Tom, Dick and Harry … and George,
    Bill and Chase … in town.

                    RITA
    That's lies. Who told you that? It
    was George. Wasn't it?

                    JOE
    What if it was? Look here. Read your
    own words. Your confessions. Right
    here!
            (Throws phone at her.)

                    RITA
            (Looks at phone.)
    That's not me! That's not me! That
    was never me!

                    JOE
          (Pushes RITA onto the
          bed. Leans over and
          begins choking RITA.)
Bitch! Whore! Slut! You're nothing
but a fucking cunt!

                    RITA
          (Gags, tries to fight back
          but is overwhelmed by
          JOE'S strength)

                    JOE
Nothing but a haj bitch-whore. Not
worth a beer-piss.

                    RITA
          (Gags, is losing
          consciousness - goes limp)

                    JOE
Fucking get what you deserve!

               (Enter OFFICER and EMILY -
               to the Apartment Door)

                    EMILY
Here! Officer! Here!

                    OFFICER
          (Pounding on door)
Police! Open this door!

                    JOE
          (Gently holding RITA)
Oh … my … God … Rita! What have I
done?

                    OFFICER
              (Pounding on door. Speaks
              into radio.)
     Backup! I need Backup!
              (Removes weapon from
              holster)
     Police! Open this door! … Police!
     I'm going to break it in.

                    JOE
              (Takes pistol from
              waistband.)
     Rita. Rita. Rita. My blessed little
     Rita. You deserved more than me.
              (Beat)
     This will fix it.
              (Puts pistol to his head.
              Pulls trigger. Shoots.
              Falls dead.)

                    OFFICER
              (Into radio. Removes
              firearm from holster.)
     Shots fired! Shots fired! I'm going
     in!
              (To Emily)
     Stay back, ma'am.
              (Kicks through door.
              Enters apartment. Finds
              RITA unconscious and JOE
              dead. Holsters firearm.
              Talks into radio.)
     Send medics! We have one down. One
     needs a medic!
              (To EMILY)
     Help me with CPR on this one!

(OFFICER and EMILY perform
CPR on RITA. Quickly, she
responds.)

RITA

Emily? What?
(Looks where Joe lays on
floor)
Joe! Oh, Joe, my sweet boy. What
happened?

OFFICER
(To RITA)
Ma'am … try and stay calm. Help is
on the way.
(To EMILY)
Who were these two? And the others
back there?

EMILY

This is Rita. That over there is
Joe.

Back on the street are Chase and
Bill. Roger's the one who's dead.
(Cries)
Once we all were friends, Officer …
close and intimate friends. Then
things all changed. We all changed.
Now we're all collateral damage.

(Action slows. All lights
dim. The actors exit
carrying the dead and
wounded.)

## ACT III
## Scene 5

Setting:    It is a week later. Only
            the Diner is lit.

At Rise:    EMILY and RITA are working
            behind the counter of the
            Restaurant Set is the
            Diner. JESSICA sits at a
            table or on a stool.


(ENTER OFFICER)

                OFFICER
Rita, I'm sorry to be the one to
bring this to you. It is a copy of
the final investigation report.
            (Hands document to RITA)
It is pretty much what we talked
about. Roger and Bill were
pretending to be you and Joe. George
led them to do it. Roger broke down
when he was outed and nearly killed
Bill before taking his own life. Joe
assaulted you before taking his own
life … probably because of PTSD.

                RITA
            (Breaks down crying)

                OFFICER
For what it's worth, ma'am, the
autopsies showed that Roger and Joe
had significant levels of blood-
alcohol. The report showed that you

                    (OFFICER Continued)
two, Bill, Jessica … and George …
were stone cold sober.

                    EMILY
What's happens now?

                    OFFICER
Not much I'm afraid. The report goes
to the district attorney's office.
I've spoken with them and they
indicated that no charges will be
filed against anyone left alive.

                    RITA
What!

                    OFFICER
Sorry. I know it sounds bad, like
that George is getting off the hook.
But the investigation shows he
didn't have anything to gain
financially by misleading Roger and
Bill. And, although his plan caused
pain, suffering and death he didn't
actually do anything illegal
himself. The DA's office believes
everything any of them put on-line
would be judged free speech
protected by the First Amendment.

                    EMILY
What about trying to get Joe screwed
out of a job? Isn't that a financial
gain?

                    OFFICER
No. I spoke with Chase and the other
hiring officials up at the plant.
George has never had a chance of
getting taken on. Every hiring
official we interviewed said his
background check did not come back
positive. Seems he indicated he was
released Honorably. Really he was
let go on a General Discharge.

                    EMILY
He told me that was the usual
classification.

                    OFFICER
That's not quite true. A General can
be given in lieu of prosecution for
behavior that is bad enough to
disqualify a person from staying in
the service but not so bad as to
warrant sending them to jail. The
key words on the discharge papers
are "Prior to ETS for the good of
the Army."

                    EMILY
So he lied about that, too. What
about what Chase posted on line?
Will he face charges?

                    OFFICER
No. It's that First Amendment
protection again. Online you can say
pretty much what you want … no
matter the truth or who gets hurt.

(OFFICER Continued)
As long as you're not trying to
solicit sex with a minor or commit
outright fraud nothing is illegal,
in this country anyway.

EMILY
Speak of the devil ... here he comes
now.

(Enter GEORGE -
Swaggering)

EMILY
Get your lying ass out of here you
miserable sack of shit!

GEORGE
Now little darlin', I'm sure the
Officer here has informed you the
investigation concluded I didn't do
anything illegal.

EMILY
Yeah, he did. I guess just being a
total immoral, lying, piece of shit
asshole isn't a crime if you have
someone else do the deed for you.

GEORGE
Now darling ...

EMILY
If you ever call me 'darling' again
I will ... will ...
                (Looks at OFFICER)

                    OFFICER
                (Waves finger 'no-no' like
                at Emily)

                    EMILY
I don't know what I'd do. Just get
your ass out of here. You and your
money aren't welcome and never will
be.

                    GEORGE
Odd thing about that, darlin', I
spoke with your boss and he assured
me otherwise. Actually, my lawyer
spoke with him, and it was a brief
conversation. My lawyer did the
talking and your boss did the
listening.
                (Points at EMILY and RITA)
You, darlin', and Rita both are in
danger of losing your jobs if you
don't serve me promptly and with all
courtesy. That's what your boss
said. And, right now, I'd like one
of you to serve me up a cup of
coffee … promptly and with all
courtesy … while I can look at those
beautiful breasts and remember days
gone by.

                    OFFICER
Sir, you are treading a fine line
here. I must advise you that
harassment can be treated as verbal
assault.

                    GEORGE
Sure. I get it. You're here to help
them not the average, taxpaying
citizens just trying to have a cup
of coffee at the corner diner.

                    RITA
Here, George, let me get it for you.
          (Takes pot of coffee and
          pours it into George's
          crotch.)

                    GEORGE
Bitch!

                    RITA
Oh, dear. Look what I did. Silly me.
I guess I was distracted by your
good looks and obvious virility.

                    GEORGE
Officer, I demand that you arrest
her for assault!

                    OFFICER
Sorry, sir, but I didn't see a
thing. You are free to all 911 and
make a report. If dispatch wants me
to address the complaint they'll
radio me.
          (Beat)
Oh, and if you do decide to exercise
your right to call you might
consider that the dispatcher on duty
right now is Bill's sister, Wanda.

GEORGE
Fuck you! Fuck all of you! Jessica,
let's get out of here.

JESSICA
I'm not going anywhere with you. Not
now, not ever … never.

GEORGE
So the whole cabal of you is
standing against me. Well, you're
not the only ones in this town.

JESSICA
Actually, there may be more of us
than you see.
          (Pats stomach)
But you won't be part of his life.

GEORGE
You're pregnant! I knew it!

JESSICA
Maybe I am and maybe I'm not. One
way or another you'll never know.

GEORGE
I knew it! I knew it! And the kid is
mine!

JESSICA
What kid? Did I say there is a child
other than you involved here? Let me
tell you something, George. If I
were pregnant with your child I
would abort it just to spite you.

(JESSICA Continued)
Abort it and make sure the whole damn world knows. There is no way in this world I'll be saddled with you the rest of my life. Not even for one more day. I've had enough of your lies and taken enough of your shit.

GEORGE
Whore! A father has rights, too!

OFFICER
Sir, once again, you're treading a fine line. I advise you to choose your words carefully. Very carefully, sir, very carefully.

GEORGE
Fuck you! You're not a part of this conversation so butt the hell out. Jessica, we are going … now!

JESSICA
You said were about to leave … but we aren't going anywhere
          (Pats stomach)

RITA
You can stay with me!

EMILY
Or me!

          (GEORGE pulls JESSICA
          towards him)

                    GEORGE
No, bitch! You're coming with me!

                    JESSICA
                (Pulls away)
No I am not. You've bullied me since
middle school and you're not going
to bully me any longer. Leave me
alone. Now!


                    OFFICER
Sir, You've crossed that line again.
For the last time, I am warning you.
Watch what you say and how you say
it … and I carefully watch where
those hands of yours end up.

                    GEORGE
                (To Rita and Emily)
You two bitches have had it in for
me since forever. You think you're
on top now … that you have Jessica
under some spell. Maybe right now
you do. But the child she's carrying
will need a father and she'll need
me soon enough. Then we'll see who
comes out on top. Yes we will. Then
we will see.


                    JESSICA
George, I do not want you to call
me, talk to me, visit me … or have
any contact with me ever again.
                (To OFFICER)
Is that a clear enough for me to
call the police if he ever comes
around?

                    OFFICER
For right now I think so. It would
be better to get a no contact order
from Judge Scoropinski tomorrow.
I'll be happy to sign as a witness
on his behavior.


                    GEORGE
<u>I told you to stay the fuck out of</u>
<u>my business!</u>


                    OFFICER
I am in the lady here's business,
sir. Not yours. Now, sir, if I were
you I'd move along. You have said
enough. All of you have said enough.
Enough people of died over this.
Everyone needs to cool down.


                    GEORGE
I told you before to fuck off and
stay out of my business. I know
people in this town. You'll regret
ever siding with these whores.
          (Beat)
Now, fucking whore bitch, <u>we're</u>
<u>leaving</u>.


              (GEORGE Takes JESSICA'S
              arm again. JESSICA pulls
              free from GEORGE'S grip.)

              (GEORGE takes JESSICA'S
              arm again and pulls her
              towards the door.)

                    JESSICA
No! I am not going with you!


                    OFFICER
Sir! You will release her right now.
Now!


                    GEORGE
Or what, you asshole! Just what are
you going to do about it? Numb-nuts!


                    OFFICER
Sir! If you do not release her and
leave now I will arrest you for
assault. You will spend at least one
night in jail. And I will enjoy
fulfilling my civic duty to take you
there.


                    GEORGE
Better call for reinforcements, fuck
head!
                    (Still is holding onto
                    Jessica's arm, pulls her
                    towards door.)


                    JESSICA
Help!


                    OFFICER
                    (Into radio)
Officer involved in an active
assault. Send backup.
                    (To GEORGE)
Sir, I order you to release your
grip and lay on the floor! Now! On
the floor!

                    GEORGE
Better wait for help, asshole!

                    (GEORGE and OFFICER
                    wrestle. GEORGE is winning
                    the scuffle. He takes the
                    OFFICER's service weapon.
                    EMILY hits GEORGE on the
                    head with a plate. He is
                    momentarily stunned.
                    OFFICER recovers, throws,
                    pins and cuffs GEORGE.
                    None too softly.)

                    OFFICER
                    (Into radio)
Officer involved takedown! Send a
Sergeant!

                    GEORGE
                    (Thrashing under OFFICER)
Assholes! You're all assholes!

                    EMILY
You're the only asshole here.

                    (OFFICER pulls GEORGE to
                    his feet, not too
                    carefully)

                    OFFICER
You are under arrest for assaulting
an Officer in the performance of his
duty.
                    (Produces Miranda card)

                (OFFICER Continued)
You have the right to remain silent.
Anything you say or do can and will
be used against you in a court of
law. You have the right to consult
an attorney before speaking to the
police and to have an attorney
present during questioning now or in
the future. If you cannot afford an
attorney, one will be appointed for
you before any questioning, if you
wish. If you decide to answer any
questions now, without an attorney
present, you will still have the
right to stop answering at any time
until you talk to an attorney.

                GEORGE
Fuck you!

                OFFICER
It will be the best piece of ass
you'll be getting for the next five
to seven years. Now, you will
accompany me to my patrol car.
Either walk voluntarily or I will be
happy to escort you.
                (To the rest of the actors
                on stage.)
A Sergeant will be here shortly to
take your statements. Please remain
until he or she releases you. If
anyone needs me, I'll be in my
patrol car writing up my report on
tonight's festivities.
                (Pushing GEORGE to exit)

(OFFICER Continued)
And, miss, I could really use a cup
of coffee.

                    EMILY
               (Holding up a to-go coffee
               cup)
Yes. How do you take it?

                    OFFICER
Black. I'll be back for it.
               (Smiling at EMILY)
Darlin'.

               (Exit OFFICER, pushing
               GEORGE)

                    RITA
Wow. … Jessica are you really
pregnant? What are you going to do?

                    JESSICA
Doctors say I am … But I'm not
sure what I'm going to do. Chase
arranged for me to work on the
plant's production line as long as I
can. That provides me enough money
to live on. My parents don't know
yet. Guess I'll have to tell them
tonight.

                    EMILY
Better they hear it from you than
from half the town tomorrow.
               (Beat)

                    (EMILY Continued)
What about you, Rita? Are you going
to take that job in LA?

                    RITA
I don't think I can right now. Joe's
mother is pretty messed up right
now. I've been spending nights at
her house. Better there than our …
my ... apartment.

                    EMILY
It looks like George succeeded in
one thing … you're screwed until you
can get this behind you. I know you
would go if you could, it's been
your dream to leave this town … and
mine to go with you.

          (Enter OFFICER)

                    OFFICER
The boy's in the back of my car.
I'll take that coffee now.

          (EMILY pours coffee and
           OFFICER sips)

                    OFFICER
Good stuff. Thanks.

                    EMILY
What's going to happen to him?

                    OFFICER
Felonious assault on Jessica,
assault on an officer in the line of

(OFFICER Continued)
duty, and I can probably gin up a
few more charges.

The boy's facing two or three years
in the gray-bar hotel. And probably
the same or more time with active
probation. What are you ladies going
to do now?

JESSICA
I have an aunt out in LA who keeps
suggesting I come live with her.
Maybe I'll do that. She has lots of
room. Rita has a job offer out there
and Emily could …

EMILY
(Interrupting, pointing
about the restaurant)
If I can work here I can work
anywhere!

OFFICER
Nothing is keeping you three tied
down here. The investigation into
what happened before is done and we
can get all the information we need
about tonight's excitement at the
station tomorrow.

(RITA, EMILY and JESSICA
nod and mumble agreement)

OFFICER
When I was at the university, one of
the profs advised our class that

(OFFICER Continued)
your twenties were the best time to take chances. That later, when you marry and have kids, your next eighteen years are pretty much settled. She said the worst that can happen is you fall flat on your face and have to move back in with your parents. And facing having to move back in with your folks at thirty … now THAT is motivation enough to succeed somehow.
            (Looks off-stage)
Well, my Sergeant is here. I've got to fill her in on what happened.
            (Nods to Emily)
Thanks for the coffee.


            (Exit OFFICER)


                  RITA
I guess I did say you could come live with me, Emily. And LA isn't that far by plane.


                  EMILY
Glad to hear it. I want to see this town in general and that asshole George …
            (Points offstage)
… well behind me and not coming looking for me.
            (Beat)
What about you, Jessica? We both gave the asshole more than we should have. I got off easy. What are you going to do?

                    JESSICA
I need to go somewhere and take the
time to think. I want to put some
space between me and him, too.
          (Beat)
Want me to call my aunt and see if
there's room for all of us? At
first, anyway, while we get settled?


                    RITA
          (Demurely)
Yes.

          (More assuredly)
Yes!

          (Throws apron on floor.)
YES!


                    EMILY
Damn straight, girlfriends! Let's
lose this town. Let's get our butts
out of this town.
          (Calls to off-stage.)
Fred! I'm out of here! The place is
all yours now. Bye.


          (Exit JESSICA, RITA and
          EMILY)

     LIGHTS/CURTAIN/BLACKOUT

          END OF PLAY

## About the Play

Common law has not kept pace with social media. Bullies rule the day from school-aged children on the playground to politicians for the highest office. Social media enables destructive behavior while the cultural norms encoded in law are no longer enforceable. Rarely, if ever, do bullies face consequences for their action. Just as rarely does society support victims.

Absent some resolution of the problem, social media will continue to support rather than sanction anti-social behavior.

I wrote an initial version this play for the 2014-15 Mario Fratti-Fred Newman Political Play Contest.

I have dedicated this work to my late, brother Paul Anthony Benson, in the hope that he's found some peace now.

## About the Author

Patrick M. Benson was born in Seattle, Washington and now lives in Flagstaff, Arizona. Mr. Benson spent forty years as an applications programmer, software engineer and systems manager before turning to creative writing.

His other works include the very technical *Database Sockets - Web Application and Development*, published in 2012. This is a examination of the technology now supporting high-speed web traffic and e-Commerce.

Another stage play, *Hearing*, received an Honorable Mention in the 2011 Writer's Digest Annual Writing Contest.

www.ingramcontent.com/pod-product-compliance
Lightning Source LLC
LaVergne TN
LVHW052029080426
835513LV00018B/2234